宣化上人開示錄

（一）

Venerable Master Hua's
Talks on Dharma

Volume One

宣化上人開示錄

（一）

英 譯

佛經翻譯委員會

出 版

法界佛教總會
佛經翻譯委員會
法界佛教大學

Venerable Master Hua's

Talks on Dharma

Volume One

English translation by the
Buddhist Text Translation Society

Buddhist Text Translation Society
Dharma Realm Buddhist University
Dharma Realm Buddhist Association
Burlingame, California U.S.A.

Published and translated by:

Buddhist Text Translation Society
1777 Murchison Drive,
Burlingame, CA 94010-4504

1994 Buddhist Text Translation Society,
Dharma Realm Buddhist University,
Dharma Realm Buddhist Association

First Chinese edition published 1984,
Dharma Realm Buddhist Books Distribution Society, as
宣化上人開示錄(一)
Xuan Hua Shang Ren Kai Shi Lu (Yi)

First bilingual edition 1994
(Second Chinese edition, First English edition)

03 02 01 00 99 98 97 96 95 94   10 9 8 7 6 5 4 3 2 1

ISBN 0-88139-025-9

Notes : Pinyin is used for the romanization of Chinese
words, except for proper names which retain
familiar romanizations.

Addresses of the Dharma Realm Buddhist Association's branch
offices are listed at the back of this book.

佛經翻譯委員會八項基本守則
The Eight Guidelines of
The Buddhist Text Translation Society

1. 從事翻譯工作者不得抱有個人的名利。
   A volunteer must free him/herself from the motives of personal fame and reputation.

2. 從事翻譯工作者不得貢高我慢，必須以虔誠恭敬的態度來工作。
   A volunteer must cultivate an attitude free from arrogance and conceit.

3. 從事翻譯工作者不得自讚毀他。
   A volunteer must refrain from aggrandizing his/her work and denigrating that of others.

4. 從事翻譯工作者不得自以為是，對他人作品吹毛求疵。
   A volunteer must not establish him/herself as the standard of correctness and suppress the work of others with his or her fault-finding.

5. 從事翻譯工作者必須以佛心為己心。
   A volunteer must take the Buddha-mind as his/her own mind.

6. 從事翻譯工作者必須運用擇法眼來辨別正確的道理。
   A volunteer must use the wisdom of Dharma-Selecting Vision to determine true principles.

7. 從事翻譯工作者必須懇請大德長老來印證其翻譯。
   A volunteer must request Virtuous Elders in the Ten Direction to certify his/her translations.

8. 從事翻譯工作者之作品在獲得印證之後，必須努力弘揚流通經、律、論以及佛書以光大佛教。
   A volunteer must endeavor to propagate the teachings by printing sutras, shastra texts, and vinaya texts when the translations are certified as being correct.

目　錄

Contents

開 經 偈
Verse for Opening a Sutra

無 上 甚 深 微 妙 法

The unsurpassed, deep, profound,
subtle, wonderful Dharma,

百 千 萬 劫 難 遭 遇

In hundreds of thousands of millions of eons,
is difficult to encounter;

我 今 見 聞 得 受 持

I now see and hear it, receive and uphold it,

願 解 如 來 眞 實 義

And I vow to fathom the Tathagata's
true and actual meaning.

佛法在行不在説

道德是爲人的根本，有了道德，
我們才能立得住腳。

光陰似箭，日月如梭，江河之水後浪推前浪，韶
華易逝，世上青年逐老年，這樣隨之逐之，漸漸
又歸於老死朽滅，無蹤無影，足見一切無常。

正因爲一切都是無常，所以我們應該趕快找一個
歸宿。在座各位，總算幸運，找來找去，終於信
佛了。信佛，能令我們得「常樂我淨」——究竟
之樂；所以我們應信佛。可是，也並不是説只是
「信」便可以了，也要依法修行，若是只信而不
修行，有如説食數寶，於自己本身了無益處。所
以古人説：

　　道是要行的，
　　不行則要道何用？
　　德是要修的，
　　不修則德從何來？

所以，我們應該躬行實踐，常把「生死」二字掛

The Buddhadharma
Is in Practice, Not in Talking

It's because the Way and virtue are a person's foundation. Once we have the Way and virtue, we can stand on our own feet.

Time is like an arrow: the days and months fly by like a shuttlecock. The waves in the river follow one after another. Glory fades quickly. In the world, youth is followed by old age. In this way, we gradually return to the decay and extinction of old age and death, leaving no trace or shadow. Clearly, everything is impermanent.

Since everything is impermanent, we should quickly find a refuge. All of you can count yourselves lucky, for you have searched around and finally come to believe in the Buddha. Faith in the Buddha enables us to attain the ultimate happiness of permanence, joy, true self, and purity. Therefore we should believe in the Buddha. But it's not enough to say that we believe. We also have to cultivate according to the Dharma. If you believe but don't cultivate, it's like talking about food without eating it, or counting the wealth of others—it doesn't benefit you in the least. So the ancients said:

> *The Way must be practiced. If it is not*
> *practiced, what use is the Way?*
> *Virtue must be cultivated. If it is not cultivated,*
> *from where does virtue come?*

We should personally practice, always hanging the words "birth"

3

在眉梢，把「道德」二字放在腳下。這一句話看起來很難懂，爲什麽說應該把「道德」二字放在腳下呢？因爲，道德二字是爲人的根本，好像樹木的根一樣，所以有了道德，我們才能立得住腳；反之，腳下無根，那麽則無處可立，進退維谷，不能有所作爲了。若是我們能把這二字實踐了，那麽，人格更可以立得住，而一切亦自然可以成功了，所以說：「道德二字，是做人的根本。」《論語》上說：「君子務本，本立而道生。」務本才能生出道，這是古有明訓的。

正如剛才所說，日子是似箭般在不知不覺間過去了，過去的且讓它過去，可是來者可追，對於未來，我們應立下宗旨，不讓它糊里糊塗地度過。

西樂園一向的宗旨是提倡「淨土法門」，主張大家精進念佛。所以每年的六月十九日和十一月十七日（中國陰曆），都照例地舉行觀音及阿彌陀佛七的念佛法會，可是呢？大家不可以就「照例參加」，馬馬虎虎地敷衍一下就算了，應該一年比一年精進，念茲在茲，在這七天裏頭，在在處處、時時刻刻我們都要勤念菩薩的名號，不可以懈怠。

and "death" on our brows, and putting the words "Way" and "virtue" beneath our feet. Maybe that's hard to understand—why should we put the words "Way" and "virtue" under our feet? Because the Way and virtue are a person's foundation. They are to us what roots are to a tree. Once we have the Way and virtue, we can stand on our own feet. But with no base under our feet, we have no place to stand. We are in a fix, unable to advance or retreat, and we cannot accomplish anything. If we can actually practice these two things, then we can establish a good character and naturally be successful in whatever we do. So it's said, "The Way and virtue are the foundation of being a person." The *Analects* of Confucius also say, "The superior person attends to the root. When the root is established, the Way comes forth." Only when the fundamentals are tended to can the Way come forth. This is wise advice from the ancients.

As mentioned earlier, the days pass as swiftly as an arrow, but we don't notice it. As for the days gone by, just let them go. Only the future is worth pursuing. We should set guidelines for the future, so we won't let the time pass in a muddle.

Western Bliss Garden Monastery has always promoted the Pure Land Dharma-door and exhorts everyone to vigorously recite the Buddha's name. Every year, on the nineteenth of the sixth lunar month and the seventeenth of the eleventh lunar month, we will continue as usual to hold Dharma Sessions for reciting the names of Guanyin Bodhisattva and Amitabha Buddha. However, everyone should certainly not just casually "attend as usual," not taking it seriously and letting it pass lightly. Rather, each year we should be more vigorous than the year before; we should work intensively. During these seven days, no matter when and where we are, we

我們要念菩薩，而不是要菩薩念我們，爲什麼說不要令菩薩念我們？因爲在這打七的期間，你若是掛打七的名，而雜念紛紛，也不勤稱誦菩薩的洪名，那麼大慈大悲的菩薩，一定會爲你這個可憐的眾生而可惜，爲你不是誠心來打七而焦急，所以大家應該至誠懇切地念，而且更進一步地要有一顆慈悲喜捨的心。如果能夠這樣，我敢肯定地說一句：「菩薩是絕對會加被各位的。」

同時，西樂園從來沒有用帖子請過任何一個，大家都是自動發心來參加打七，這點可見大家並不是沒有誠心，而這種自動發心的精神，也很值得嘉許。既然這樣，我們更不要讓這分真誠白費了，我們都要發願念個「水落石出」，念至菩薩現身說法，才不枉這次參加打七一場。

今天是打七的第一天，在這開始打七的今天，我預祝各位今年能有所成就，否則，我要和大家算帳，要是帳算不清，可別後悔！閒話不多講了，還是多念幾句菩薩的洪名吧！

一九五八年觀音七 六月十三日上午開示於香港西樂園寺

6

should diligently be reciting the Bodhisattva s name and never become lax .

We should be mindful of the Bodhisattva; it's not that the Bodhisattva should be mindful of us. Why don't we want the Bodhisattva to be mindful of us? If you are nominally participating in this session, but in fact a lot of idle thoughts are keeping you from being diligent in reciting the Bodhisattva's vast name, the Bodhisattva of Great Kindness and Compassion will certainly take pity on you, this poor living being, and be worried because you are not sincerely participating in the session. Therefore, everyone should earnestly and sincerely recite, and go a step further by nurturing kindness, compassion, joy, and renunciation in your mind. If you can do that, then I guarantee that the Bodhisattva will aid and support you.

Moreover, everyone has come to the session of his own free will; Western Bliss Garden Monastery has never sent invitations to anyone. This shows that everyone is certainly not lacking in sincerity. This spirit of initiative is very commendable. Therefore, we shouldn't let this sincerity go to waste. We should all vow to recite until "stones peep out from the receding water" (the truth is brought to light), until the Bodhisattvas appear before us to speak the Dharma; then, we will not have come to the session in vain.

This is the first day of the session. On this day, I bless you all and wish you success this year. If you don't have any success, I will have to settle accounts with everyone. And if your account isn't cleared up, you will be sorry. I won't chatter too much; we had better recite the Bodhisattva's vast name some more!

A talk given on the morning of June 13,1958, during a Guanyin Session at
Western Bliss Garden Monastery in Hong Kong.

大悲咒能消災難

眞正的好處，是説不出來的，
如人飲水，冷暖自知。

在天氣炎熱中，大家能不畏熱，也不怕山高路遠
地趕來參加打七，究竟有什麽好處？眞正的好處
，是説不出來的，如人飲水，冷暖自知，唯有眞
心的人，才能自然而然地領會到其中的妙處。

怎麽樣才能獲得好處呢？沒有其他，正如方才所
說，只要眞心地念菩薩的名號。眞心，換句話來
說就是專心；所謂「專一則靈，分歧則弊」，能
夠專一，就自然能夠感應道交，這種感應道交的
力量，是不可思議的，可是這卻要自己用功，旁
人無法代替你，更不是可以僥倖得到的。

就拿「說食數寶」作一個譬喻，譬如一個人，光
是説吃飯怎麽樣有營養，可是始終都不去吃，那
麽，飯縱使眞有營養，而說的人能得到它的營養
嗎？所謂：

The Great Compassion Mantra Can Dispel Calamities

One cannot speak of true advantages. It is just as someone will know the warmth or coolness of a glass of water only after drinking from it.

Despite the hot weather, people have not been put off and have rushed here to attend the session, undaunted by the long journey and arduous climb. Ultimately, what advantages does this have? One cannot speak of true advantages. Just as someone will know the warmth or coolness of a glass of water only after drinking from it, true-hearted people will naturally understand the wonder in this.

How can one obtain the advantages? There's no way aside from what I just said—you must recite the Bodhisattva's name with a true heart. A true heart is just a concentrated mind. It is said, "When one is concentrated, it is efficacious. When one is scattered, there is nothing." If you can be single-minded, you will obtain a spontaneous response in the Way. The power of the response in the Way is inconceivable. However, you must apply the effort yourself; no one can do it for you, and even less can you attain it by chance.

Consider the example of "talking about food and counting others' wealth." If someone talks about how nutritious the food is, but doesn't eat it, then even if it really is nutritious, how can the person get the nutrition? It is said:

　　　　終日數他寶，自無半錢分；
　　　　於法不修行，其過亦如是。

我們念菩薩，也是這個樣子，不能只是知道，或談論念菩薩的功德就算了，我們要能真正地念到一心不亂，甚至於，更進一步地連水流、風動，在我們的耳中聽來，也無不是稱誦菩薩洪名的聲音，所謂：

　　　　有情無情，
　　　　同演摩訶妙法。

如果不能做到這一地步，不能一心不亂的話，那麼，各相雜陳，風吹就是呼呼聲，水流就是淙淙聲，就不能領略其中的妙處了。所以，我們應真實地念，而且在念的時候，不要摻入其他的妄念，這樣才能夠獲得其中的法益。

其次，在打七時，應該重視打七的規矩，所謂「無規矩不能成方圓」。至於西樂園一向的規矩，就是不得喧嘩吵鬧，以免障礙他人的修行。

在這七天的期間，我們又念〈大悲咒〉。這個〈

All day long you count the money of others,
But you don't own half a cent yourself.
If you don't cultivate the Dharma,
You make the same mistake.

It is also the same when we recite the Bodhisattva's name. If we just know and talk about the merit and virtue of reciting the Bodhisattva's name, it doesn't count. We have to truly recite until we are single-minded and unconfused, and even further, until the sounds of the water and wind in our ears are just the recitation of the Bodhisattva's vast name. It is said,

Sentient creatures and insentient things,
All proclaim the wonderful Dharma
    of the Mahayana.

If you have not reached that level of being single-minded and unconfused, then everything will be jumbled together. When the wind blows, you just hear a whooshing sound; when the water flows, you just hear the roaring sound. You cannot perceive the wonder in it. So we should honestly recite and not let any idle thoughts mingle in our recitation. Only then can we derive the benefits of the Dharma.

This time when we hold the session, we should pay attention to the rules for the session. As it is said, without a compass and a ruler, you can't draw circles and squares. The traditional rule of this temple is to avoid causing a disturbance, so that you won't hinder others from cultivating.

During these seven days, we will also recite the Great Compassion

大悲咒〉的功德，是不可思議的，如果沒有相當善根，就連「大悲咒」這三個字，也不能輕易聽到，現在大家不但能聞其名，而且更能受持讀誦，足見各位具大善根，曾於諸佛所種諸善根了，既然有大善根，那麼大家便不可輕易空過此生。

記得最初在西樂園打七，居士十有八九是不會念〈大悲咒〉的，可是，到了今天，十個裏有八個以上都會念了，這就是諸位居士們顯著的進步。現在我說一段故事，來證明〈大悲咒〉的功德：

在我們東北地方，有一個財主，他擁有很多田產，有一年的秋天，這個財主他親自隨著四、五輛大貨車，滿載著高粱到市上去賣。因為鄉間和城市的距離有一百五十多里路，所以，他在凌晨一時多，就趕車起程，可是在半途中，不幸遇賊，那財主見前面有賊，就念起〈大悲咒〉，說也奇怪，那幫土匪竟然像瞎子一樣，看不見他的車，於是乎，他們便安全渡過難關，這是我所見聞〈大悲咒〉的靈感之一。

《大悲心陀羅尼經》上說：「誦持大悲咒者。能

Mantra. The merit and virtue of the Great Compassion Mantra is inconceivable. Without considerable good roots, it's not easy to even hear the three words "Great Compassion Mantra." Now everyone can not only hear the name, but also uphold and recite it. That proves that you all have tremendous good roots, which you planted when there were Buddhas in the world. Since you have such great good roots, you should not casually let this life go to waste.

I remember that when the temple held the first sessions, eight or nine out of ten laypeople didn't know how to recite the Great Compassion Mantra. And now, eight or more out of ten laypeople can recite it. That shows the progress made by the laity. Now I'll tell a story which proves the merit and virtue of the Great Compassion Mantra.

In Manchuria, there was once a wealthy man who owned a great deal of land. One autumn, he accompanied four or five large cargo trucks carrying full loads of sorghum to be sold in the city. Since the city was over a hundred and fifty *li* from the village, he started out at a little past one o'clock in the morning. Unfortunately, he ran into some bandits on the road. Seeing them up ahead, the rich man started reciting the Great Compassion Mantra. Strangely enough, the gang of bandits were just like blind men and didn't notice his trucks at all. Thus, they passed safely through the difficulty. That's one of the efficacious responses of the Great Compassion Mantra that I have personally heard about.

In the *Great Compassion Mind Dharani Sutra*, it says, "Those who recite the Great Compassion Mantra can dispel all disasters. They will not be burned by fire or drowned by water." So I urge the

消諸難。遇火不焚。遇水不溺。」所以，我勸已
經會念的居士，每日應最少誦持三遍，至於不會
念的，也應趕快學。誦持〈大悲咒〉的功德，不
但能退盜賊，更能消除百病，平諸魔難，所以我
們應該誠心地誦持。

在這開始打七的今日，法會的氣氛很好，很能鄭
重其事，希望各位再接再勵，更圖精進！

一九五八年六月十三日下午開示於香港西樂園寺

laypeople who can already recite it to do so at least three times a day. Those who cannot recite it should learn quickly. The merit and virtue of the Great Compassion Mantra can not only make thieves and robbers go away, it can also dispel the myriad illnesses, and resolve all demonic troubles. So we should sincerely recite it.

On this starting day of the session, there is a very optimistic spirit in the Dharma Assembly, and everyone is taking it very seriously. I hope everyone will make a determined effort, and strive to be ever more vigorous.

A talk given on the afternoon of June 13, 1958, at
Western Bliss Garden Monastery in Hong Kong

極樂世界在眼前

只要肯努力精進，
我們仍是可以「歸去」的！

「歸去來兮，田園將蕪胡不歸，既自以心爲形役
，奚惆悵而獨悲？悟已往之不諫，知來者之可追
；實迷途其未遠，覺今是而昨非。」

這幾句話，是五柳先生（陶淵明）所說的，可是
不知道他在說這幾句話時，是不是眞的能夠了悟
到其中的意義？因爲按照佛法來說，他這幾句話
是極爲契理的。

什麼是「歸去來兮」呢？我們知道，自性法身，
是從十方諸佛常寂光中流露出來，經上說：「一
切眾生皆有佛性」，我們的自性，是與諸佛無異
無別的，若是不這樣，就不能稱爲「皆有佛性」
了。我們現在不能了悟自性，這是因爲我們染雜

The Land of Ultimate Bliss Is Right Before Our Eyes

We only need persist in our vigor, and we can certainly "go home."

"I am going home! My fields and gardens are choked with weeds. Why should I not return? My mind has been my body's slave; how sad and lamentable! I realize that the past is gone, but I can certainly rectify what is to come. I have not actually strayed too far from the path. I have awakened to today's rights and yesterday's wrongs."

These sentences were spoken by Mr. Wuliu (Tao Yuanming). But I don't know whether at the time he spoke these words he had truly enlightened to their meaning, because, when regarded in the light of the Buddhadharma, these sentences tally with the ultimate principle.

What does "I am going home" mean? We know that the self-nature of the Dharma body comes forth from the constantly tranquil light of the Buddhas of the ten directions. The sutras say, "All living beings have the Buddha nature." Our basic nature is not different from, not distinct from, the Buddha. If it were not this way, then it would not be said that "all have the Buddha nature." Now we are unable to understand and become enlightened to our self-nature because we are defiled and scattered by the five desires and the wearisome dust of the Saha world. We turn our backs on

了這個娑婆世界的塵勞五欲，以至於背覺合塵，所以便不能了悟自心，識見本性。

可是我們千萬不能就這樣顛倒沈淪，應該返本還原，背塵合覺，所以說「歸去」，意思是叫我們恢復自家的本來面目，或者仗著佛、菩薩的願力，念誦佛菩薩名號的功德而得生淨土，這也可以稱爲「歸去」。

在已悟自心，已生淨土之後，發大願心，倒駕慈航來救度眾生，這就叫「來」。那麼，「田園將蕪胡不歸」中的田園，又是指什麼而言呢？田，就是說「心田」，這個道理很淺顯的，我們平常聽人說：「茅塞頓開」，若是我們不好好地修心，那麼，雜念叢生，好像田園裏頭長滿了茅草一樣，把大好的心田都荒蕪了，這就是「茅塞不開」，再也不能返本還原，明心見性了。

「胡不歸」，這三個字，是十方諸佛、一切聖人苦口婆心之語，他們都說：「可憐愚癡的眾生啊！你爲什麼不快些回頭是岸呢？」

enlightenment and join with the dust. Therefore we cannot awaken to our own minds and recognize our own basic natures.

But we certainly should not continue to be so submerged and upside-down. We should return to our source: we should turn our backs on the dust and unite with enlightenment. Therefore, the words "going home" remind us to return to our original face, to our original home. Also, perhaps, the words "going home" can mean we rely on the strength of a Buddha or Bodhisattva; by means of the merit of reciting that Buddha's or Bodhisattva's name, we can be born in the Pure Land.

After one has awakened to one's own nature and been born in the Land of Ultimate Bliss, one makes great vows of one's own to launch the ship of compassion and come back to the Saha world to rescue living beings This is what is meant by "coming back again." In the line. "My fields and gardens are choked with weeds," what do the "fields and gardens" refer to? "Fields" refer to the field of the mind. The principle here is very obvious. We often use the phrase "suddenly clear away the underbrush" to refer to the gaining of new insight. If we do not cultivate the mind well. our minds become a thicket of scattered thoughts. just as fields and gardens become overgrown with grass and weeds if not tended. These scattered thoughts choke the good field of the mind. As long as you have not "cleared away the underbrush." you cannot return to the source or understand your mind and see your nature.

"Why should I not return?" This sentence is a gentle remonstration by the Buddhas and sages of the ten directions. They say, "How pitiful and foolish living beings are! Why don't they hurry up and turn their heads around to see the other shore?"

「心爲形役」，就是說眾生既著六塵之境，不能了悟自心，所以處處都被塵境所轉；爲吃的奔馳，爲利忘軀，流轉於生死的苦海中，受種種的苦，所以萬悲俱生，苦不堪言，這又是「惆悵而獨悲」的意義了。

那麼，我們這一般眾生，是不是註定無藥可救呢？註定永遠陷於六道輪迴的深淵呢？絕對不是的。過去的，雖然錯了，可是我們還可以寄望於將來，應知「來者可追」。

在未來的日子裏，我們更不能像以往一樣地背覺合塵，心爲形役了，以前的一切不信因果、不勤修行、造業、殺生等等，都是不對的；而今日的打七、念佛，卻是對的。所以我們應該「覺今是而昨非」，對於善的，便要保留；對於惡的，立刻痛加悔改。古人說：「一寸光陰一寸金」，其實，在我們修行人的眼中，一寸光陰簡直就是我們的一寸命；少了一寸光陰，就等於我們短了一寸命一樣。

"My mind has been my body's slave." This means that living beings are attached to an environment composed of the six defiling objects—the objects of the senses—and cannot awaken to their own minds. So they are continually being turned by defiling objects; they race about feeding themselves and are intent upon making a profit up to the moment that their bodies give out. We undergo numerous sufferings as we toss and turn in the bitter sea of birth and death. Myriad agonies well up, and the suffering is unspeakable. This is also what is meant by "how sad and lamentable!"

Is it the case that we living beings are beyond salvation? Is it the case that we must wallow in the deep abyss of the turning wheel of the six paths forever? Absolutely not! Although we made mistakes in the past, there is still hope for the future. You should know that you "can certainly rectify what is to come."

In the future, we absolutely will not turn our backs on enlightenment and join with the dust, as we did in the past. Nor will we let our minds be a slave to our bodies. Everything we did in the past, such as not believing in cause and effect, not cultivating diligently, and creating the karma of killing and other offenses, was wrong. Now today, we are in this session reciting the Bodhisattva's name. This is what is right. So we should "awaken to today's rights and yesterday's wrongs." We should carefully protect what is good and immediately and firmly reform of what is bad. An ancient author said, "An inch of time is worth an inch of gold." Actually, in the eyes of a cultivator, an inch of time is worth an inch of life. For every moment that passes it is just as if our life is shortened by an inch.

是日已過，命亦隨減；

大眾！當勤精進，如救頭然。

要改惡遷善的，趕快吧！我們「實迷途其未遠」，極樂世界在望了！只要肯努力精進，我們仍是可以「歸去」的！

一九五八年六月十四日上午開示

This day is already passed,
and life is consequently shorter.
Everyone should diligently cultivate,
as if trying to save his very head.

If we wish to change our errors and tend towards the good, we should do so quicky! We "have not actually strayed too far from the path"; we can still reform. The Land of Ultimate Bliss is within sight! We only need persist in our vigor, and we can certainly "go home."

A talk given on the morning of June 14, 1958

懺悔就是改過自新

如果能眞正生出懺悔心，
也未嘗沒有商量之處。

佛之「法力」極大，而眾生的「業力」卻與之相
等，所以說凡夫是「業重情迷」，而佛卻是「業
盡情空」，所以聖、凡之分，在於「業」是不是
已經盡了，「情」是不是已經空了。又說：

覺者，佛也；
迷者，眾生。

就好像上午所說的，眾生因爲背覺合塵，被一切
塵勞五欲所轉，所以業障愈來愈深，而佛能超脫
一切五欲塵勞，不再造業。眾生因爲業重的緣故
，所以凡是想成佛了道的，必須先要懺悔自己的
罪業，如果不生懺悔心就想成佛，這就猶如「煮
沙成飯」，雖然煮到恆河沙那麼多的劫，也不可
能成功的。

24

To Repent and Reform Means to Change Our Faults and Turn Over a New Leaf

If one is truly repentant, it can certainly be worked out.

The Dharma-power of the Buddhas is tremendous, and yet the karma of living beings is equal to it. Thus living beings are said to be "weighed down by karma and confused by emotions," whereas the Buddhas "have ended their karma and emptied their emotions." So the difference between a sage and a commoner lies in whether one can end karma and empty out emotions. Another saying goes,

> *Enlightened, one is a Buddha.*
> *Confused, one is a living being.*

As we mentioned earlier, since living beings turn their backs on enlightenment and unite with defilement, being turned by the wearisome defilement of the five desires, their karmic obstacles become deeper and deeper. On the other hand, the Buddhas can transcend the sordid defilements of the five desires and avoid creating additional karma. Because living beings have such heavy karma, one who wishes to become a Buddha and realize the Way must first repent of his karmic offenses. If one hopes to become a Buddha without being repentant, it's like cooking sand and hoping to get rice. You can cook for as many eons as there are sands in the Ganges River, but you'll never succeed.

所謂「懺」，是懺其前愆；對以往所犯的罪業生大慚愧心。「悔」，是悔其後過；立定主意，改過自新，永遠不再犯錯，正如袁了凡居士所說：

> 以前種種，譬如昨日死；
> 以後種種，譬如今日生。

如果我們不勤懺悔，那麼，我們所造的罪業，就會使我們墮落，不知「伊於胡底，莫知所止」了。凡是佛教徒都會記得，在皈依時，把自己的姓名報上後，便懺悔說：

> 從於無始。以至今生。
> 毀壞三寶。作一闡提。
> 謗大乘經。斷學般若。
> 弒害父母。出佛身血。
> 污僧伽藍。破他梵行。
> 焚毀塔寺。盜用僧物。
> 起諸邪見。撥無因果。
> 狎近惡友。違背良師。……

現在，為了重新喚回大家的記憶，我且把這段〈

"Repentance" means repenting of past errors, feeling a great sense of shame and remorse for the transgressions we made in the past. "Reform" means turning away from future errors, resolving to turn over a new leaf, and never making those mistakes again. This is just what the layman Yuan Liaofan said,

> *Regard everything in the past as*
> *if you died yesterday.*
> *Regard everything in the future as*
> *if you were born today.*

If we don't repent with diligence, then the karma from the offenses we committed will make us fall, and who knows when and where we will stop. All Buddhists should remember that when they first took refuge, they stated their full name and then repented by saying the following:

> *From time without beginning until the present life,*
> *I have slandered the Triple Jewel, been an icchantika,*
> *Slandered the Great Vehicle Sutras,*
> *Cut off the study of Prajna,*
> *Killed my father and mother,*
>   *shed the Buddha's blood,*
> *Defiled the Sangharama,*
> *Ruined the pure conduct of others,*
> *Burned and wrecked stupas and temples,*
> *Stolen the property of the Sangha,*
> *Held deviant views, denied cause and effect,*
> *Been intimate with evil friends,*
> *Turned away from good teachers...*

懺悔文〉，很簡單地向大家解釋一下：

我們從無始劫以來，直至現在，所做的罪業，真是不可勝數。第一，是毀謗佛、法、僧三寶，其中又以毀謗「僧寶」的罪爲最大，因爲僧人是代表佛陀來傳揚佛法的，所以，謗僧的罪是「不通懺悔」的。什麼叫「闡提」？這是梵語，翻譯成中文是「信不具」或「無善根」；譬如你對這種人說法，他不歡喜聽，甚至於乾脆就說：「我不信！」你說，這是不是把自己的善根都給斷送了呢？

「謗大乘經」，就是誹謗大乘經典；譬如有人說佛經的道理是假的，或者說大乘經是魔王所說的等等，這也是一種「不通懺悔」的罪行。至於「般若」也是梵語，翻譯成中文是「智慧」。般若，又分實相般若、觀照般若、文字般若三種，可是無論哪一種都好，若是斷學（不去學），就會愚癡。愚癡的果報，是會淪爲畜生道。

「弒害父母」，這一句包含了殺阿羅漢和殺聖人的罪；譬如，提婆達多殺四果阿羅漢，這就是其中的一個例子。

Now, to refresh everyone's memory, I will very briefly explain this passage of repentance for everyone.

From eons without beginning, up to today, the karma from the offenses we have committed cannot be reckoned. First of all, we have slandered the Triple Jewel: the Buddha, the Dharma, and the Sangha. Among these, the offense of slandering the Sangha is the gravest, because the members of the Sangha represent the Buddha in propagating and transmitting the Buddhadharma. Therefore, one is not allowed to eradicate the offense of slandering the Sangha through repentance. What is an "icchantika"? It's a Sanskrit word which means "incomplete faith" and "lacking good roots." If you try to speak the Dharma to these people, they don't want to listen. They may even tell you straight out, "I don't believe it." Wouldn't you say they've cut off all their good roots?

"Slandered the Great Vehicle Sutras" means, for instance, saying that the principles in the Buddhist Sutras are false, that the Great Vehicle Sutras were spoken by demon kings, and so forth. This sort of offense cannot be pardoned through repentance. "Prajna" is also Sanskrit and means "wisdom." There are three kinds of Prajna: Real Mark Prajna, Contemplative Prajna, and Literary Prajna. If you don't study any kind of Prajna, you will be stupid. The retribution of stupidity is that you will fall into the destiny of animals.

"Killed my father and mother" also includes the offenses of killing an Arhat and killing a sage. One example is Devadatta killing a Fourth Stage Arhat.

其次，「出佛身血」，也是一種「不通懺悔」的罪過，可是有許多人誤解了，以為這只是指佛在世時，用刀割截佛陀的身體，才算是犯了這條罪行。其實在佛滅度後，凡是有毀壞佛像者，都算在內；譬如故意去剝落佛像的金漆、損毀佛像等都是。雖然，這不是損害佛的肉體，可是，這個罪卻和用刀宰割佛的真身一樣。

「污僧伽藍」，是指褻瀆了寺門梵寺；譬如，在寺廟上住的在家夫婦，若在廟內做出不正當的事，吃肉殺生等等。至於「破他梵行」，是引誘本來清淨不染的出家人破犯戒律，這也是「不通懺悔」的。

「焚毀塔寺」的意義很明顯，就是說焚燒及毀壞寺門佛刹；譬如，昔日馮玉祥火燒白馬寺和少林寺等。「盜用僧物」，就是用不正當的手段來奪取常住的財物，這種人心裏所存的，都是一些邪知邪見，自以為是，常常說著無因果的曲調，於是倒行逆施，無惡不作，無所不為，這樣又怎能不墮落呢？

最後，要說到「狎近惡友，違背良師」了，「惡

Next, "shedding the Buddha's blood" is also an offense for which repentance is not accepted. Many people wrongly think this offense only means actually cutting the Buddha's body with a knife when the Buddha was in the world. In fact, after the Buddha entered Nirvana, damaging Buddha images in any way also counts as this kind of offense. This includes peeling the gold paint off the Buddha images, ruining Buddha images, and so forth. Although this does not harm the Buddha physically, it is equivalent to cutting the Buddha's body with a knife.

"Defiling the Sangharama" means profaning the pure temple. An example would be if married couples living on temple grounds engage in indecent activities, eat meat, kill living creatures, and so on. "Ruining the pure conduct of others" means inducing left-home people who were pure and undefiled to break the precepts. Repentance is not allowed for this either.

"Burning and wrecking stupas and temples" means setting fire to and damaging Buddhist temples, just as Feng Yuxiang set fire to White Horse Monastery and Shaolin Monastery in the past. "Stealing the property of the Sangha" means using improper methods to seize the wealth and property of the permanent dwelling. The people who do that all hold deviant knowledge and views. They think they are right, and they insist that there is no cause and effect. Acting rebelliously, they stop at no evil. There's nothing they won't do. How can they not fall?

Finally, we'll talk about "being intimate with evil friends, and turning away from good teachers." In Confucianism, evil friends

友」，在儒家稱爲「損友」，好像時下的「阿飛」，以及黑社會的人物等，我們都不應該與之爲伍，因爲這都是惡友之類。有些人交上了這些損友，就漸入歧途，不聽師長的勸告，爲非作歹，黑白不分，冠履倒置，你說多麼可憐！

以上所說的這種種罪愆，都是非常要不得，但卻很容易犯的，那麼，若是不幸地已經犯了又怎樣呢？也不要灰心，所謂「彌天大罪，一懺便消。」罪，本來是無形的，如果能眞正生出懺悔心，也未嘗沒有商量之處。大家切不可自暴自棄，自甘墮落啊！

一九五八年六月十四日下午開示

are called "harmful friends." For example, we should not associate with tramps, gangsters, and so forth, because they are considered evil friends. Some people associate with such harmful friends and gradually stray onto the wrong road themselves. Refusing to listen to their teachers' exhortations, they will do all kinds of evil. They can't tell the difference between right and wrong, and they act in upside-down ways. Wouldn't you say they are pitiful?

The various offenses mentioned above are all extremely serious, yet very easy to commit. If one has unfortunately committed them already, what should be done? Don't be disheartened, because "Offenses may fill the skies. Repent, and they disappear." Offenses have no shape or form, and if one is truly repentant, it can certainly be worked out. No one should give up on himself and be resigned to falling!

A talk given on the afternoon of June 14, 1958

教他作，罪加三級

無論在誰的面前懺悔，要把話說得
清楚，不要說些模稜兩可的話。

昨天我曾很簡單地對大家解說一段〈懺悔
文〉，只是解釋到「狎近惡友，違背良師」，現在，我
繼續把它說下去：

「自作教他」我們知道無論殺、盜、淫、妄、酒
，都是不正當的行為，而每種罪業，又分有因、
緣、法、業四種，譬如說殺吧，殺有「殺因」、
「殺緣」、「殺法」、「殺業」，無論哪一種，
又都離不了「自作」或「教他作」。

「自作」，就是不假手旁人，親自去做不正當的
事。「教他作」，就是鼓勵和教唆別人去做不正
當的事，這種間接犯罪的方法，比直接的還要罪
加一等，因為它在已有的罪上還加上狡詐的罪行
，所以「自作」固然有罪，而「教他作」的罪行
更大。

34

Telling Others to Do Something Increases the Severity of the Offense

No matter in front of whom we are repenting, we must say our confession clearly. Don't be vague and vacillating.

Yesterday I briefly explained part of the repentance text for everyone, but I only explained up to "being intimate with evil friends and turning away from good teachers." Now I will continue to explain further:

"I have done these myself, told others to do them, and rejoiced at seeing and hearing them done." We know that killing, stealing, sexual misconduct, lying, and taking intoxicants are improper ways to behave. Each of those offenses are divided into four aspects: causes, conditions, dharmas, and karma. For example, with killing there are the causes of killing, the conditions of killing, the dharmas of killing, and the karma of killing. In any of these aspects, one either personally commits the offense, or tells someone else to do it.

"Doing them oneself" means that instead of putting it into someone else's hands, one personally engages in the improper deed. "Telling others to do them" means encouraging and inciting others to do improper things. This way of indirectly committing an offense is more serious than directly committing it, because the offense of fraud is added to the original offense. Thus, if you do it yourself, it's already an offense, but if you tell others to do it, the offense is even greater.

什麼是「見聞隨喜」呢？就是知道別人在犯罪，而幫助他去犯，這就是古人所說的「助紂為虐」，我們試閉目想想，從無始劫以來，我們究竟犯了多少次這樣的罪？我想不用說得那麼久遠，就在我們短短的一生中，所犯的也就不可勝數了。

所以〈懺悔文〉接著又說：「如是等罪。無量無邊。」我們的罪是算數之所不能及，也可以說是大到無有邊際的。既然知道了自己罪深障重，那麼，我們應該怎樣做才對呢？不用說，自然應該在佛前至誠懇切地懺悔。

所以〈懺悔文〉又說：「故於今日。生大慚愧。克誠披露。求哀懺悔。」「克誠」二字，是懺悔的時候所必須具有的心。有些人對師父懺悔，非常地馬虎，常常藏頭露尾地把過錯給遮掩，這表示他並沒有誠意來懺悔自己的過失，像這樣的懺悔，就算歷盡百千萬億恆河沙劫，也不能把罪業消除乾淨的。

所謂「直心是道場」，我們無論在誰的面前懺悔，也要把話說得清楚，不要說一些個模稜兩可的話。譬如，問他有沒有犯過這種過失，他就說「

What is "rejoicing at seeing and hearing it done?" It means you know someone else is committing an offense, and you help him to do it. The ancients called this "aiding the wicked King Zhou to do evil," that is, adding bad to worse. We should close our eyes and think about it: since eons without beginning, just how many times have we created these offenses? We don't even need to talk about such a distant time. In this short life alone, we have already made uncountable transgressions.

So the repentance continues, "All such offenses, limitless and boundless..." Our offenses are not only beyond reckoning, they are indeed vast beyond all bounds. Now that we realize how deep our offenses are and how serious our obstructions are, what should we do? Without being told, you should naturally know to go repent sincerely before the Buddhas.

Thus the repentance text continues, "Therefore on this day, I bring forth great shame and remorse, confess sincerely, and seek to repent and reform." In repentance, sincerity is essential. Some people are very casual about it when they repent to their teacher. They give only a partial account, covering up or glossing over their mistakes. This shows that they are not really sincere about repenting of their errors. If that's how they repent, then even after as many eons as there are sands in a hundred million Ganges Rivers, the karma of their offenses will not be cancelled.

It's said, "The straight mind is the Way-place." No matter in front of whom we are repenting, we must say our confession clearly. Don't be vague and vacillating. For example, if you ask someone if he has ever committed a certain offense, he says, "I don't

不記得」，或者說「可能有」等等，這種不徹底的懺悔，不但不能消除罪業，反而會種下惡因，因為佛法是絲毫也不能馬虎的。可是有些人也會說：「某某人做了哪些惡業，可是現在卻飛黃騰達，是不是沒有因果，沒有公理？」有一首偈頌這樣說：

> 縱使百千劫，所作業不亡；
> 因緣會遇時，果報還自受。

由此可知，造業是必有報應的，只是時間的問題，看看因緣是否會合罷了。

有人又會說：「縱使百千劫，所作業不亡；那麼，是不是沒有辦法消除罪障了呢？」也不是沒有辦法，辦法就是「惟願三寶。慈悲攝受。放淨光明。照觸我身。」希望佛、法、僧三寶，能夠本著慈悲的大願，用清淨無礙的大光明，照觸到我們的身上，這種淨光照後，能令我們三障消除，如雲開見月般，復現出我們本來的清淨心性，所以說：「諸惡消滅。三障蠲除。復本心源。究竟清淨。」

remember," "I might have," or the like. Instead of eradicating the karma of one's offenses, that kind of superficial repentance only plants evil causes, because in the Buddhadharma, one cannot be the slightest bit careless. Some people will always bring up certain examples, such as, "So-and-so created all that bad karma, but now he's so successful. Does that mean there's no cause and effect? Is there no justice?" There's a verse which goes:

> *Even in a hundred thousand eons,*
> *The karma you create does not perish.*
> *When the conditions come together,*
> *You must still undergo the retribution yourself.*

From this, we know the karma we create is sure to bring a result, a corresponding retribution. It's only a question of time; it depends on whether the conditions have come together or not.

Now someone may ask, "If it's the case that 'even in a hundred thousand eons, the karma you create does not perish,' then is there no way to eradicate the karma of our offenses?" There is a way, which is to say: "I only hope the Triple Jewel will compassionately gather me in, and emit a pure light to shine on my body." That is, one hopes the Triple Jewel—the Buddha, the Dharma, and the Sangha—will, in their great vows of compassion, shine their pure, unobstructed, great radiance upon our bodies. When this pure light shines on us, it can remove the three obstructions and reveal our original pure mind and nature, just as the clouds disperse to reveal the moon. Then we conclude the repentance by saying, "All evil is extinguished, and the three obstructions are cast out. I return to the original mind-source, and am ultimately pure."

說完了這首〈懺悔文〉以後，我希望大家都能明白不懺悔的害處，和能懺悔的益處。另外，還有一首〈懺悔文〉這樣說：

> 往昔所造諸惡業，皆由無始貪瞋癡；
> 從身語意之所生，一切我今皆懺悔。

這首〈懺悔文〉不但能懺悔罪障，而且能把我們所以造罪的原因說出來，所以我希望每個人天天都能在佛前，誠心地念誦三遍或數遍。現在，我也把它略略解說一下：

「往昔」，就是以前。近的以前是今生的以前，遠的以前是無始劫以來，在這往昔的時光中，我們不但出牛胎，入馬腹，一時姓張，一時姓李，輪轉於六道之內，而且在這段時間中，我們又不知造了多少罪業。

爲什麼我們會造罪呢？〈懺悔文〉中說得清楚，「皆由無始貪瞋癡」，這意念上的貪、瞋、癡三毒，就是萌發無數罪業的根由。還有因爲這三毒的作祟，我們的身體又做出了殺、盜、淫三業，

Now that I've explained this repentance text, I hope everyone understands the harm of not repenting, and the benefits of being able to repent. Another verse of repentance says:

> *For all the bad karma created in the past,*
> *Based upon beginningless greed, hatred*
>   *and stupidity,*
> *And born of body, mouth and mind,*
> *I now repent and reform.*

This verse of repentance not only allows us to repent of our offenses which have become obstructions, it also explains what caused us to create those offenses. So I hope everyone can sincerely recite it before the Buddhas each day, three times or limitless times. Now I will briefly explain it.

"In the past" includes the recent past, which is this life, and the distant past, which extends back to eons without beginning. In our past lives, we have turned in the six paths, leaving a cow's womb, entering a horse's womb, sometimes born in the Smith family, sometimes born in the Jones family. During all that time, who knows how much karma we created with our offenses?

Why do we commit offenses? The repentance verse says very clearly that it's "based upon beginningless greed, hatred and stupidity." The three poisons of greed, hatred and stupidity in the mind are the root cause from which immeasurable karma of offenses stems. And due to the evil influence of the three poisons, our bodies engage in the karma of killing, stealing, and sexual misconduct. In our speech, we engage in lying, frivolous talk,

41

在語言上也產生了妄語、綺語、惡口、兩舌等罪，所以文中又說：「從身、語、意之所生。」

無論是身體上犯的殺、盜、淫三業也好，還是語言上所犯的妄語、綺語、惡口、兩舌也好，或者是在意念上所犯的貪、瞋、癡也好，我們都要懇切地懺悔，否則會如入泥沼，愈陷愈深，罪業愈來愈重，把我們壓得喘不過氣，無能自拔。

在座各位都具上上的善根，我相信大家都會不忘懺悔，而一定能夠發願把罪業懺悔和消除盡的。

一九五八年六月十五日上午開示

scolding, backbiting, and so on. Thus the verse says, "And born of body, mouth and mind."

Whether it's the three offenses of killing, stealing, and sexual misconduct which we commit with our bodies, or the lying, frivolous talk, scolding, and backbiting committed in our speech, or the greed, hatred and stupidity in our minds, we must sincerely repent of them all. Otherwise, we will be as if caught in quicksand, sinking deeper as the karma from our offenses grows heavier. We will be buried until we can't breathe, unable to pull ourselves out.

Everyone here has supreme good roots. I believe no one will forget to repent, and everyone will make a vow to repent of and eradicate all the karma of their offenses.

A talk given on the morning of June 15, 1958

修行有四個階段

皈依那天，看作我們的生日，
把我們修行的階段從那時候算起。

一年裏頭有「春、夏、秋、冬」這四季，這是人人所知道的事，然而大家是不是知道，在人生的路程上，也分爲「生、老、病、死」這四個階段？因爲誰也免不了一死，所以，我們應好好地爲自己的身後歸宿打算一下，這就要修道了。從修行方面來説，也可分爲「學、行、成、了」四個階段：

人生由一至二十歲，可説是「學道」的時期，在這段時間，我們應好好地讀書，或學佛法，這就等於《大學》中所説的「在明明德」一樣，這時應把自己的光明德性弄明白。二十一至四十歲，是「行道」的時期，應該學以致用，把以前所學的，所明白的，用以普渡眾生，匡扶世俗，這是《大學》中所説的「在親民」。

The Four Stages of Cultivation

We could consider the day we took refuge as our birthday, and start counting the stages of our cultivation from there.

In one year, there are the four seasons of spring, summer, fall and winter—that's common knowledge. But does everyone know that the journey of life is also divided into the four stages of birth, old age, sickness, and death? Since no one can avoid death, we should seriously be thinking about where we will go when our life ends. That means we have to cultivate the Way. Cultivation can also be divided into four stages: study, practice, attainment, and full realization.

The period from ages one to twenty can be considered the period of studying the Way. During this interval, we should be diligent in our academic studies or in our study of the Buddhadharma. This is equivalent to "illumining the bright virtue" spoken of in *The Great Learning*. At this time we should have a clear understanding of our bright inherent virtue. From the ages of twenty-one to forty is the period of practicing the Way. We should put what we have learned, what we have understood, into practice, in order to extensively save living beings and reform the world. In *The Great Learning,* this is called "renewing the people."

From the ages of forty-one to sixty is the period of "attaining the

四十一至六十歲，便到了「成道」的時候，這是《大學》中所說的「止於至善」。可是孔子所說的「至善」並不徹底，並不能達到眞空、涅槃的境界，並不是究竟的，所以我們還要「了道」。在成道以後歸於涅槃的境界，這要比儒教的三綱領：「明德、親民、止於至善」更爲圓融了。

也許有人會這樣說：「我在一到二十歲的時期中還未信佛，這樣說來學道的時期已經過去了，那麼是不是沒有機會學，也不用學了呢？」可是，我們要明白，方才所說的四個階段的年期，只是一種理想，這並不是硬性的規定，所以我們可以把皈依那天，看作我們的生日，把我們修行的階段從那時候算起。

有些人又說：「我皈依了四、五年，可是一點佛法也沒學到。」其實你皈依了四、五年，在佛教裏只不過是一個四、五歲的小孩罷了！所以，我們不用引以爲憾，說自己沒有用。佛法深奧，只要你在皈依的二十年中努力去學道，那不是一樣能有所成就嗎？

Way." This is spoken of in *The Great Learning* as "resting in the highest excellence." However, what Confucius called "resting in the highest excellence" still isn't the end, for it doesn't reach the state of true emptiness and Nirvana. It's not ultimate. Therefore, we still have to achieve the full realization of the Way. After attaining the Way, we must still return to the state of Nirvana, which is more all-encompassing than the three Confucian principles of illumining virtue, renewing the people, and resting in the highest excellence.

Maybe some people will say, "When I was between the ages of one and twenty, I wasn't a Buddhist yet. Since the period for studying the Way has already passed, does it mean I have no chance to study, and that I don't need to study?" Well, you should understand that the ages for the four stages mentioned above are just ideals, not rigid definitions. So we could consider the day we took refuge as our birthday, and start counting the stages of our cultivation from there.

Some people say, "I took refuge four or five years ago, but I haven't learned any Buddhadharma at all." Actually, if you took refuge four or five years ago, you're merely a four or five year-old child in Buddhism. So there's no reason for us to lament that we're useless or that the Buddhadharma is too deep and abstruse. After you take refuge, if you diligently study the Way for the first twenty years, and diligently practice the Way for the next twenty years, won't you have achievements just the same?

Perhaps the older generation of laypeople will sigh, "I'm already eighty, and may not live for that many more twenty years!" You are

　　或者老一輩的居士又會感慨地說：「我現在已八十歲囉！恐怕沒有機會二十年又二十年地活下去吧？」一點也不錯，「時光減處命光微」，時日確是無多了，那麼你也可以把時間縮短了來算，譬如兩個月修道，兩個月行道，如此類推，只要肯下真心與決心，老當益壯，精進勇猛地一步一步做去，也是可以成功的，努力吧！

一九五八年六月十五日下午開示

absolutely right, for "As time gets shorter, life is slipping away." Indeed, there's not much time left, so you can shrink the time. For example, you can study the Way for two months, practice the Way for two months, and so on. As long as you are sincere and determined, growing younger with the years, proceeding step by step with vigor and courage, you can also succeed, so work hard!

A talk given on the afternoon of June 15, 1958

早起晚睡爲誰忙

我們要夙興夜寐地去禮佛、念佛，
爲求消滅罪障，爲法忙。

> 夙興夜寐爲誰忙？
> 眾生難度頗堪傷；
> 迷諸塵勞性顛倒，
> 耳提面命化無方。

夙興，是早起；夜寐，是夜眠，有很多人就就業
業，早起夜眠，爲的是什麼？究竟是爲我忙呢？
還是爲你忙呢？還是爲他忙呢？這個問題，我相
信很多人都無法回答，甚至於有人索性就說：「
無事忙！」

啊！那可奇怪了。然而卻偏偏有人去做連自己也
不清楚的事；譬如商人，他們一天到晚都想著自
己的「生意」，弄到睡也睡得不安眠，這就是夙
興夜寐爲「錢」忙，乃至於士、農、工、商，凡

Rising Early and Retiring Late, for Whom Are We Busy?

From morning till night, we should bow to the Buddhas and recite the Buddhas' names to eradicate our obstructions from offenses, and we should be busy for the sake of the Dharma.

> *Rising up early in the morning, going to bed late*
> *at night, for whom are we busy?*
> *Living beings are hard to save: it's pretty sad.*
> *Confused by the wearisome dust,*
> *their natures are upside-down.*
> *Boxing their ears and commanding them directly,*
> *there is still no way to teach them.*

Getting up early in the morning and going to bed late at night, many people are busy all day doing all kinds of work. For the sake of whom? In the last analysis, is the person busy for the sake of himself? Is he busy for your sake? Or is he busy for the sake of others? I believe that a lot of people can't come up with a satisfactory answer to this question; even to the point that some people make a point of flippantly saying "busy doin' nothin'."

Ha! That's strange. But indeed, there are people who do things without really knowing why. For example, some people spend every waking moment intent upon their business, almost to the point of perpetual insomnia. This is being busy from morning till night for the sake of money. And so it is with scholarship, farming, laboring, business: if we want any accomplishment, then we can't do as we

是想成功的，便會不由自主地要「朝起早，夜眠
遲」了。

《詩經》裏有這麼一段：

> 雞既鳴矣，朝既盈矣，
> 匪雞則鳴，蒼蠅之聲。

這幾句話，如果照普通的口氣來說，就是「雞好
像已經啼了吧！現在已是早上了嗎？啊！原來不
是雞在啼，只不過是蒼蠅的聲音罷了！」這段《
詩經》是形容古代的賢明君主。你看，身為皇帝
，晚上尚且不得好睡，整晚惦記著只要天亮了便
應臨朝理事，以致神經過敏地把蒼蠅的聲音聽為
雞在鳴叫，這就是夙興夜寐為「民」忙了。所謂
「一人有慶，兆民賴之。」若是遇著了這樣賢明
的仁君，老百姓就可以過著刀槍入庫、馬放南山
的幸福生活。那麼，身為君主的，難道可以不夙
興夜寐地為人民謀幸福嗎？

至於我們修道的人，也要夙興夜寐，既不是為利
忙，也不是為名忙，而是為「法」忙。我們要「

please or be our own boss, but instead we must get up early and retire late.

As a passage from the *Book of Odes* says,

> *The cock has already crowed!*
> *The morn is already full!*
> *Oh, that's not that cock that's crowed*
> *It's just the buzzing of a fly.*

In ordinary language, we could paraphrase the poem, "It seems that the cock has already crowed. Is it morning already? Oh! That wasn't the cock crowing, it was just the sound of a fly buzzing." This is describing one of the virtuous and wise emperors of old. As an emperor, he didn't sleep easily at night. The whole night long, he thought of nothing but the dawn, when he could get on with the day's business. In his anxiety for the night to pass, he rested so fitfully that he started at the sound of a buzzing fly and mistook it for the cock's crow. This is an instance of being busy from morning till night for the sake of the people. It is said, "If there is a single man with blessings, the masses will put their trust in him." If there is a humane ruler who is worthy and intelligent, the populace will be able to put away their weapons, let their horses out to the pasture, and live in peace. However, the emperor himself must rise early and retire late, working for the prosperity of the people. How can he not do that?

We who cultivate the Way should also be busy from morning till night, not for the sake of profit, nor for the sake of fame, but for the sake of the Dharma. We should "serve the Buddhas without laxness in the morning and evening." We should get up early in the morning

夙興夜寐，以事諸佛。」要朝起早、夜眠遲地日日禮佛誦經，表示我們是個忠實、誠摯的佛教徒，並不是口是心非，能說而不能做的。

況且禮佛，又包含了專一其心，恭敬其身的意思，並且禮佛更能消除業障，所謂「佛前頂禮，滅罪恆沙。」罪，幸虧是無形的，若是有形的東西，便會把恆河沙那麼多的世界都充滿了，所以，我們要夙興夜寐地去禮佛、念佛，爲求消滅罪障，爲法忙。

可是眾生的品性，是極其難測的，譬如他歡喜吃甜的，給他酸的便不高興；歡喜酸的而給他甜的，他也不高興。諸如此類，若是不認識眾生的性，就無法去度眾生了。可是佛有智慧，他能夠熟知眾生的根性，所以便能隨類應化，時常奔走跋涉，不辭勞苦地去度眾生。不過眾生並不因此而感動，反而不肯接受佛、菩薩的度化，所以說：「眾生難度頗堪傷」，傷就是悲傷，爲了眾生的愚昧顛倒而悲傷；佛菩薩是常常生大悲心的。

and go to bed late at night, and every day bow to the Buddhas and recite sutras to display our devotion and sincerity as Buddhist disciples. It should not be that we say the right things but our hearts are false. It should not be that we can talk but not practice.

When we bow to the Buddhas, we should concentrate single-mindedly and show respect with our bodies. Bowing to the Buddhas can eradicate obstructions which result from offenses. It is said, "To bow before the Buddhas can eradicate offenses as numerous as the grains of sand in the Ganges." It is a good thing offenses are formless. If they were solid objects they would fill up worlds as numerous as the Ganges' sands. Therefore, from morning till night, we should bow to the Buddhas and recite the Buddhas' names to eradicate our obstructions from offenses, and we should be busy for the sake of the Dharma.

But living beings' dispositions are extremely difficult to fathom. For instance, if they like to eat sweets and you give them something sour, it makes them unhappy. But on the other hand, if you give sweet things to people who like to eat sour things, then they get upset. That's the way they all are. If you don't understand each individual's disposition, you will have no way to save people. Only the Buddha's wisdom is sufficient to be familiar with living beings' basic natures, and because of that, the Buddha can offer teaching that is appropriate to each one. He constantly travels and roams about, accepting toil and suffering in order to save living beings. But even that doesn't suffice to move living beings. They still will not accept the teachings of the Buddhas and Bodhisattvas. So it is said, "Living beings are hard to save: it's pretty sad." "Sad" means deep regard to the point of grief. Because living beings are so stupid and upside-down, the Buddhas and Bodhisattvas constantly give rise to hearts of great compassion on their behalf.

為什麼眾生會這樣難度呢？「迷諸塵勞性顛倒」
，這就是一個答案。因為眾生在無量劫裏頭深染
六塵，於是便在苦海中，頭出頭沒，輾轉沈淪，
弄得顛顛倒倒，以苦為樂，以非為是。譬如現在
的人，明明知道服裝太時髦了，就不莊嚴，也會
生出不良的後果來，可是呢？人人都明知故犯，
互相比賽競爭，卻不知道「苦海無邊，回頭是岸
。」又譬如戰爭中所用的武器，人類不但不把它
消滅，反而「精益求精」，努力尋求發明一些愈
多愈妙的殺人武器。你說！這不是顛倒是什麼？

為了眾生的顛倒，一切聖人、善知識都苦口婆心
地諄諄勸導我們這般可憐的眾生，像長輩提著小
輩的耳朵來當面訓導一樣，可是呢？眾生卻置若
罔聞，甚至還千方百計地隱瞞自己的罪過，不被
師長們知曉，這真是「耳提面命化無方」了。

啊！眾生犯罪的本領，可謂至矣！盡矣！連佛、
菩薩也感到難以化度我們這般可憐的眾生，你說
這不是很值得悲哀嗎？

一九五八年六月十六日上午開示

Why are living beings so hard to save? "Confused by the wearisome dust, their natures are upside-down." That's one answer. Because throughout limitless eons, living beings have become deeply stained by the six defiling objects, the six dusts, they constantly bob around in the sea of suffering, sinking, thrashing, totally upside-down. They take suffering for bliss and the false for the true. Thus people of today become so caught up in "fashion," that even when the current styles are unattractive and may lead to undesirable reactions, they still compete to stay in fashion. People don't know that the sea of suffering is boundless, but a turn of the head is the other shore. Take military weapons for instance: not only do people fail to get rid of them, they seek to break their own records. Great effort is exerted as they seek to invent new weapons for killing people—the more outrageous the better. If that isn't upside-down, what is?

In order to put an end to living beings' upside-downness, sages and wise advisors earnestly admonish us and repeat their exhortations over and over in order to guide us pitiful creatures. They are like elders who pull on the ears of their youngsters and admonish them directly. But living beings ignore those messages as if they hadn't even heard them, to the point that they employ thousands of methods and hundreds of schemes to hide away their offenses so their teachers and elders won't find out about them. This is truly a case of "boxing their ears and commanding them directly, there is still no way to teach them."

Ah! The talent living beings have for committing offenses is truly endless! Even the Buddhas and Bodhisattvas feel it is hard to save us pitiful creatures. What a sad situation!

A talk given on the morning of June 16, 1958

念佛如同打電話

如果你自己不打電話，
又有誰來接你的電話？

念念眞誠念念通，
默默感應默默中；
直至山窮水盡處，
逍遙法界任西東。

剛才所說的偈頌，大家能否了悟其中的眞義？

「念念眞誠念念通」：第一個念，是心中所發出
的念。第二個念，是有之於心，而形之於口，從
口中發出的；若只存有第二念，口念的「念」，
便不能算是眞誠的念了，所以「心」、「口」俱
要眞誠，這是對念菩薩或念佛而言。我們要念到
心口合一，一而不二。我們不可隨便地念，也不
可散亂地念，也不可夾雜其他的妄想來念，如果
能做到這幾點，便可以稱爲「眞誠」了。

Reciting the Buddha's Name Is Like Making a Phone Call

If you don't make the call, then who's going to answer the phone?

> *Thought after thought is true and sincere;*
> *thought after thought penetrates.*
> *Working quietly, there's a response*
> *in the midst of the quiet work.*
> *Go straight to the place beyond the*
> *mountains and streams,*
> *And you will be free to roam the Dharma Realm,*
> *going east or west as you please.*

Has everyone awakened to the true meaning of the above verse?

The first "thought" refers to the thought produced from the mind. The second thought comes from the mouth. It originates in the mind and takes form in the mouth. If you only keep the secondary thought of the mouth, it doesn't count as a thought of true sincerity. Therefore, the mind and the mouth must both be sincere in reciting the name of the Buddha or Bodhisattva. We should recite until the mind and mouth unite into one, and are no longer two. We should not recite casually or with a scattered mind, nor should we entertain idle thoughts while reciting. If we can fulfill these conditions, then we can be considered sincere.

有了真誠的意念，一定會有感應的，這感應是什麼呢？就是凡夫的心和佛菩薩的光相通，所謂：

> 光光相照，
> 孔孔相通。

為什麼會有這種感應呢？譬如打電話，號碼打通了，對方一聲「喂！」於是乎就可以暢所欲言，有了連絡。念菩薩聖號也如同撥電話號碼，到時菩薩就會問你：「善男子（善女人），你想求些什麼？」於是你就可以有求必應了。若是沒有誠心，這就好像是五個號碼，你只撥三個號碼就住手了，那又怎能把電話打通呢？念菩薩亦復如此。假使你念一會兒又不念了，這就沒有誠意，那是一定不會通的。

這種光光相照的感應，是只有身受的人才能感覺到的。譬如打電話，也只有拿起聽筒收聽的人才能清楚對方的話，凡夫的肉眼是無法看到聲波的去來，所以說：「默默感應默默中」。

「山窮水盡」是「百尺竿頭重進步，撒手天空另

idle thoughts while reciting. If we can fulfill these conditions, then we can be considered sincere.

If our thoughts are sincere, we will certainly obtain a response. What kind of response? Our common mind will interpenetrate with the light of the Buddhas and Bodhisattvas, as in the saying,

> *The lights shine upon one another;*
> *The holes mutually connect.*

Why will such a response occur? It's like making a phone call: after you dial the number, the other person answers, "Hello?" Then you can say what you need to say and communicate with each other. Reciting the Bodhisattva's name is like dialing the number. Then the Bodhisattva will ask you, "Good man (Good woman), what do you seek?" At that point, you will obtain whatever you seek. But if you aren't sincere, it will be like dialing only three digits of a five-digit phone number. How can the call go through? Reciting the Bodhisattva's name is the same. If you recite for a while and then stop because you lack sincerity, your recitation certainly won't go through.

The response of lights shining upon one another can only be felt by the people who personally do it. Similarly, when there's a phone call, you have to pick up the receiver in order to hear the caller clearly, because the eyes of ordinary people cannot see the sound waves. So it is said, "Working quietly, there's a response in the midst of the quiet work."

有天。」的境界，念至山窮水盡時，簡直是念而
不念，打成一團、念成一片了，那時就可以「逍
遙法界任西東」。若是我們要往生西方極樂世界
，就可以應念而往；若想倒駕慈航，回來廣度眾
生，也可以應念而回到極樂世界之東的娑婆世界
，乃至一切法界，也皆可應念而往，所以說「任
西東」，所謂：

> 一如意一切如意，
> 一自在一切自在。

所以我們學佛，處處要真誠，不然便是虛偽，虛
偽便會「開謊花，不結果」，所以學佛切記不要
自己騙自己。

其次，古人也說：「君子求諸己，小人求諸人。
」我們不可有依賴心，應知感應是自己所招，並
非從外得來的。有人說：「念佛得生淨土，是仗
佛力所接引。」此話可以說是對，也可以說是不
對，為什麼？因為「接引」這個說法，只是對機
而言；因為眾生的貪，都是希望能用力少而收效
大，好像放高利貸，放出的少，而收入的多，所

"Beyond the mountains and streams" refers to the state of: "At the top of a hundred-foot pole, take another step. Let go in midair and another world appears."

When you recite to the point that the mountains and streams have vanished, you are basically reciting, yet not reciting. You are reciting with a single mind, in a state of uninterrupted mindfulness. At that time, "you will be free to roam the Dharma Realm, going east or west as you please." If we want to be reborn in the Land of Ultimate Bliss in the West, we can recite and obtain the response of being reborn there. If we want to turn the ship of kindness around and come back to save living beings on a vast scale, we can also recite and obtain the response of returning to the Saha world, east of the Land of Ultimate Bliss. In general, we can recite and obtain the response of going to any Dharma Realm. So the verse says, "going east or west as you please." It is said,

When one wish is fulfilled,
all wishes are fulfilled.
When we are at ease in one place,
we are at ease everywhere.

Therefore in studying Buddhism, we must always be sincere. If we are false, then we are nothing but "sterile blossoms that don't bear fruit." So in the practice of Buddhism, take care not to cheat yourself.

Furthermore, the ancients have said, "The superior person makes demands on himself. The petty person makes demands on others." We should not be dependent on others. We should recognize that responses result from our own efforts; they don't come from

以聖人隨機應變，說出了佛力接引的話，目的是叫一切眾生努力去念。其實他們念佛、菩薩的名號而能往生淨土，也是全憑自己的力量，怎麼說呢？

念佛是佛替你念的嗎？你念菩薩的那個念，是菩薩生出來的嗎？如果不是，又豈能說是仗他力？譬如佛菩薩放光加被你，這也是你自己念佛菩薩的功德所感。再拿打電話作一個例子，如果你自己不打電話，又有誰來接你的電話？所以念佛也是這個道理。

其實有這種希望仗佛力接引而生淨土的心，就是貪心，就是依賴，是要不得的。我們修行要仗自力，打起精神，鼓起勇氣，勇猛精進，應知果報並不是人家能夠賜與的，所以念佛也可以說不是仗佛力所接引。

古人又說：「將相本無種，男兒當自強。」我們學佛，也要挺起胸膛來這樣說：

a provisional explanation spoken for greedy living beings who hope to put in a little effort and obtain a lot. This is like loan sharks that give a little and take in a lot. The sages accommodated the potentials of living beings and said that the Buddha's power leads us, with the goal of making living beings recite vigorously. In reality, when they recite the names of the Buddhas or Bodhisattvas, they are relying on their own strength to obtain rebirth in the Pure Land. How is this the case?

When you recite the Buddha's name, does the Buddha recite for you? Does the thought of reciting the Bodhisattvas' names come from the Bodhisattvas? If not, then how can you say you rely on an external strength? For example, when the Buddhas and Bodhisattvas bestow aid by shining their light on you, that's also in response to your efforts in reciting the names of the Buddhas and Bodhisattvas. Consider the analogy of a phone call again. If you don't make the call, then who's going to answer the phone? The same principle applies to reciting the Buddha's name.

Actually, hoping the Buddha's power will lead us to rebirth in the Pure Land is just greed and dependency, and we don't want that. In cultivation, we want to rely on our own strength, rouse our spirits, pluck up courage, and vigorously advance. Know that rewards and retributions cannot be given to you by others. Therefore, when we recite the Buddha's name, we're not really relying on the Buddha's power to lead us.

The ancients also said, "No man is a general or prime minister by birth. One must rely on his own effort to obtain such a position." We who study Buddhism should stand up tall and say,

> 佛陀本無種，
> 眾生當自強。

若是不這麼樣，整日依賴佛力接引，猶如富家子弟依賴父兄遺業，終會把自己害了，大家應該趕快猛醒啊！

一九五八年六月十六日下午開示

No one is a Buddha by birth.
A living being must rely on his own
  effort to achieve Buddhahood.

If you don't do this, but instead rely on the Buddha's power all day long, you are just like the children of rich families who depend on what they inherit from their parents and older brothers. In the end, you only hurt yourself. Everyone should quickly wake up!

A talk given on the afternoon of June 16, 1958

毋臨渴而掘井

誰叫你自己在沒病的時候，
任作胡爲，不好好地珍惜自己。

病後始知身是苦，
死後方知錯用心。

這是眾生的通病，在沒有病時，滿以爲在世間非
常快樂和滿足，到有病的時候，不能動，也不能
吃，一切都不自由了，再加上種種難以忍受的痛
苦，才覺得原來這個身體是令我們苦的，可是呢
？已經太遲了。所謂：

臨崖勒馬收韁晚，
船到江心補漏遲。

誰叫你自己在沒病的時候，任作胡爲，不好好地
珍惜自己。病是這樣，生死大事也是這樣。

「死後方知錯用心」，平時不加檢點，等到見了
閻王時，才知自己生前所行所事及存心都不正當

Don't Wait Till You're Thirsty to Dig a Well

Who told you to act so recklessly and brashly when you were free of sickness, instead of cherishing and taking care of yourself?

> *Only after being sick do you realize*
> *the body is suffering.*
> *Only after dying do you realize*
> *you applied your effort wrongly.*

Living beings all have this problem. When you are not sick, you think the world is a happy and satisfying place. But when you get sick, you cannot move around, eat, or have the freedom to do what you want, and you endure all kinds of unbearable pain and misery. That's when you discover that this body actually causes us a lot of suffering, but it's already too late. As it is said,

> *When the horse is on the edge of the cliff,*
> *it's too late to draw in the the reins.*
> *When the boat is in the middle of the river,*
> *it's too late to patch the leaks.*

Who told you to act so recklessly and brashly when you were free of sickness, instead of cherishing and taking care of yourself? This is true not only with sickness, but also with the great matter of birth and death.

69

。生前看見別人念佛，自己反而去譏謗他，說他迷信，笑他愚癡，但現在後悔已晚了！刀山油鑊之苦，都是自己招來的。就像剛才所說「臨崖勒馬收韁晚，船到江心補漏遲」，誰叫自己事前沒有準備？

所以朱子說：「宜未雨而綢繆，毋臨渴而掘井。」我們在未下雨時，早就應該顧慮到下雨時可能發生的事。譬如北方的窗戶，都是用紙糊的，所以在未下雨時，就應把窗紙糊好，省得雨水濺濕了屋內的東西；若是等到下雨時才趕忙去糊窗，那未免太遲了一點。又好像在窮鄉僻壤的地方，沒有自來水管的設備，所以你在蓋房子時，就要考慮水源的問題；若是到了渴時，才記得去掘井，那不是太晚了嗎？

我們學佛的人，都明白一切無常，不免一死。可是！為什麼不為自己的「死」先下一番工夫呢？所謂：

> 若要人不死，
> 先下死工夫。

"Only after dying do you realize you applied your effort wrongly." During ordinary times, you failed to examine and rectify yourself. But when you see King Yama, you realize that everything you have done in your life, and all your intentions, were improper. When you saw people reciting the Buddha's name, you slandered them, called them superstitious, and laughed at them for being fools. But now it's too late for regrets. You have brought the suffering of the Mountain of Knives and the Cauldron of Oil upon yourself. As it was said above, "When the horse is on the edge of the cliff, it's too late to draw in the the reins. When the boat is in the middle of the river, it's too late to patch the leaks." Who told you not to prepare ahead of time?

So Zhuzi said, "Make preparations before it rains. Don't wait until you're thirsty to dig a well." Long before it starts to rain, we should consider the problems that might occur when it rains. For example, in northern China we use paper windows. Before it rains, we have to make sure the paper windows are pasted up well, so the rain will not wet the things inside the house. If we wait until it rains and then rush to paste up the windows, it's a bit too late. Also, in poor villages where there is no running water, you have to consider the water source when you build a house. If you wait until you're thirsty to dig a well, isn't it too late?

When we study Buddhism, we understand that all things are impermanent and death is inevitable. So why don't we first spend some time to look into the problem of our own death? It's said,

> *If you don't want to die,*
> *You must first work "dead hard."*

死工夫，就是譬如今天的打七念菩薩名號。我們打七，第一，是為求世界和平；第二，是為自己的身後打算，這就是「未雨而綢繆」了。我們打七要年年參加，不可中斷，這樣才能與阿彌陀佛、觀世音菩薩結大因緣。我們必須念到好像阿彌陀佛是我們的師父，觀世音菩薩好像是我們的朋友一樣親切，既然能做佛的弟子，做菩薩的朋友，而且能年年月月日日都是如此，自然會成為老友了。這樣，佛、菩薩一定會在我們臨命終時，接引我們到西方淨土去的，這點大家切莫懷疑。所謂：

修道之人心莫疑，
疑心一起便途迷。

我們聽善知識的話，不應該存有半點疑心。譬如善知識說：「修行要下苦功。」你就應該相信。若是你能信得徹底，那麼你一定可以明心見性，返本還原。所以我們要常聽善知識的開導，他教你「念佛」，你就應該依教來念佛；善知識他叫你「不要任性」，你就不要任性。這就是修道的要訣。

Working "dead hard" is just like joining this session to recite the Bodhisattva's name. We are holding this session first of all to pray for world peace, and secondly, to prepare for our future after this life. This is just to "Make preparations before it rains." We should participate in this session every year. Don't skip a year. Then we will have great affinities with Amitabha Buddha and Guanyin Bodhisattva. We should recite until we see Amitabha Buddha as our teacher and Guanyin Bodhisattva as our close friend. If we can be the Buddha's disciple and the Bodhisattva's friend year after year, month after month, and day after day, we will naturally become old pals. Then when our life is about to end, the Buddha and Bodhisattva will surely come to lead us to the Pure Land in the West. No one should have doubts about it. It is said,

> *Cultivators should be careful not to doubt.*
> *Once they doubt, they will be lost.*

When we listen to a Good and Wise Advisor, we should not be the least bit skeptical. For example, if the Good and Wise Advisor says that cultivation requires arduous effort, you should truly believe it. If you believe completely, you will surely be able to understand the mind and see the nature, return to the origin and go back to the source. Therefore, we should always listen to the instructions of a Good and Wise Advisor. If he tells you to recite the Buddha's name, you should follow the instruction and recite. If he tells you not to be stubborn, then don't be stubborn. This is the essential secret of cultivation.

Earlier we said, "Only after being sick do you realize the body is suffering." If people don't go through some pain and suffering, they

方才說：「病後始知身是苦」，可是呢？人若是不經過一番的病苦，是絕不肯發心修行的；因為在沒病時，他不知痛苦。

又有一句話說：「富貴學道難」，若是一個人很富有，那麼他樣樣如意，你叫他如何會想修道呢？所以，貧病都是我們修道的助緣。病來了，也不必憂；貧來了，也不用愁。有一首偈頌這樣說：

> 我見他人死，
> 我心熱如火；
> 不是熱他人，
> 看看輪到我。

自己貧、病，固然應增長修道的心，就是看見別人貧病老死，也要引以為惕。人生有如「長江後浪推前浪」，若能及時發願往生，則事前有個準備，不至臨時手足無措，手忙腳亂了。好像國家若不經過一番變亂，人民都會耽娛愛樂，不曉得愛國衛土。現在的佛教也是如此，現在的人都不謀復興佛教，所以佛教便顯得萎靡。

will not want to cultivate, because they don't know what pain is if they have never been sick.

It's also said, "It's hard for the rich and honorable to cultivate." If a person is wealthy, he can have everything the way he wants, so why should he want to cultivate? So poverty and illnesses are all aiding conditions to our cultivation. When we get sick, there's no need to be depressed. If we're poor, there's no reason to be worried. There's a verse which goes,

> *When I see someone die,*
> *My heart burns like fire.*
> *It's not burning because of him,*
> *But because I know it will soon be my turn.*

If we are poor or sick ourselves, of course we should quickly resolve to cultivate. If we see others who are poor, sick, aging and dying, we should also take it as a warning. Life is like a succession of waves. If we can make a vow to be reborn, then we will be prepared in advance. We won't be in a frantic scramble when it comes time to die. It is just like if a country hasn't passed through times of disorder, the people will indulge in pleasures, and not know that they should be patriotic and defend their country. That's the situation Buddhism is in right now. Currently no one is working to make Buddhism prosper, so Buddhism seems rather low in spirit.

We should realize that it is not only the Bhikshus and Bhikshunis who are responsible for promoting Buddhism. It is the responsibility of every Buddhist. If each and every one of us can take up the responsibility, how can we worry that Buddhism will not thrive?

要知道提倡佛教，責任不單單在比丘或比丘尼身上，而是在每一個佛教徒的身上，若是我們每個人都這樣引咎自責，那麼，還愁佛教不發展嗎？現在有些佛教徒以為佛教不及外教時髦，所以不敢對人說自己是個佛教徒，甚至於還附和別人說佛教是迷信的，你說，這樣可悲不可悲？譬如九龍的道風山上有一個外道的團體，專門收容那些佛教的比丘及比丘尼，經過他們一番「改造」之後，那些忘本的人竟然毀謗佛教。

所以真心信佛的人，應寧死不變，提起勇氣來，不可因為別人的譏笑或利誘而變志。如果每個人都不忘記自己是個佛教徒，那麼佛教復興是必然的。

一般的外道雖然目前盛極一時，可是天道循環，物極必反，大家切不可被外表的興衰而動搖自己的心志啊！真理是不滅的，佛教的復興全憑大家的努力！

一九五八年六月十七日上午開示

But now, there are some Buddhists who think Buddhism is not as fashionable as other religions, so they don't dare to tell anyone they are Buddhist. In fact, they even agree with others that Buddhism is mere superstition. Isn't that pathetic? For example, there's a non-Buddhist group at Daofeng Shan in Jiulung (Hong Kong) which specializes in accepting Buddhist monks and nuns. After they are brainwashed, they forget their roots and actually slander Buddhism.

People who truly believe in Buddhism would rather die than change their faith. We should pluck up our courage, and not let our resolve waver even if others make fun of us or tempt us. If every Buddhist remembers that he is a Buddhist, Buddhism will naturally prosper again.

Although other religions may experience temporary prosperity, the way of Heaven is a cycle, and when one extreme is reached, things turn around. No one should let their resolve be influenced by superficial signs of prosperity or decline. The truth is never extinguished. The flourishing of Buddhism depends on everyone's hard work!

A talk given on the morning of June 17, 1958

念菩薩能明心見性

眾生的心性，本來也是磊落光明，
只是被無數的罪障、妄念遮蔽罷了。

歡喜快樂，而厭惡痛苦，這是眾生的習性。然而，因為眾生是愚癡的，他們不知道怎樣才可以獲得他們所歡喜的快樂，脫離他們所厭惡的痛苦。所以，雖然眾生口裏，老是喊著尋求快樂的口號，可是很不幸地，卻愈來愈痛苦。

菩薩是慈悲的先覺者，他知道怎樣才可以離苦得樂，面對著一般可憐的苦惱眾生，菩薩便本著大悲的心腸，發出了聞聲救苦的宏誓。所以，我們眾生，也不是完全沒有希望。只要我們至誠懇切地念誦「南無觀世音菩薩」的名號，菩薩便會用他無邊的法力，度脫我們，使我們離苦得樂。這種樂，是究竟之樂，是西方的極樂。換句話說，念菩薩的名號，不但能夠脫離世間一切痛苦，並且能夠往生極樂世界，花開見佛，得到「常樂我淨」的清淨和究竟之樂。

Recite the Bodhisattva's Name to Understand the Mind and See the Nature

The minds and natures of living beings are originally clear and bright, but they've been covered over by countless obstructions from offenses and idle thoughts.

By nature, living beings like happiness and loathe suffering. But because of their stupidity, living beings do not know how to attain the bliss they crave and to leave the suffering they dislike. Therefore, although they always say they are "pursuing happiness," unfortunately they only receive more and more suffering.

Bodhisattvas are kind and compassionate beings who have already become enlightened. They understand the way to leave suffering and attain bliss. Seeing all the pitiful, afflicted living beings, the greatly compassionate Bodhisattvas vow to listen to their sounds and save them from suffering. And so living beings are not totally without hope. If we sincerely recite the great name of Guanyin Bodhisattva, he will save us with his limitless Dharma-power, and enable us to leave suffering and attain bliss—this kind of bliss is the ultimate bliss of the Western Land. By reciting the Bodhisattva's great name, not only can we transcend all the pain and suffering of this world, we can also be reborn in the Land of Ultimate Bliss, see the Buddha when our flower opens, and attain the pure and ultimate happiness of permanence, bliss, true self, and purity.

It is said that by reciting the Bodhisattva's name, we can leave suffering and understand our own mind and nature—is it really that

念菩薩就能離苦，就能了悟心性，恐怕沒有這樣便宜的事情吧！多疑的鈍根眾生，也許會這樣地問，可是呢？菩薩就是立志要做便宜眾生的事；所以，才說出這個方便的法門。然而有些眾生，連這種絕頂便宜也不知道，這是多麼可惜啊！

有些人又會說：「念菩薩的名號，能消罪除苦，這點我相信，可是為什麼念菩薩的名號，也能使我們明心見性？」幾天前，我曾說過「打電話」的譬喻，現在我再說一個更簡單的比喻吧！

譬如，一個人被蒙上了眼睛，於是乎他就覺得四周都是漆黑一片，走起路來，到處碰壁，碰得焦頭爛額，苦不堪言，可是自己卻不曉得解除眼睛上的束縛。幸好遇著一個慈悲的人，看見他這副可憐相，便走上前，替他除下眼睛上的束縛。所以，這個曾經看不見的人，現在可以看見了，不再痛苦，也不會到處碰壁。

「念菩薩能明心見性」的道理也是這樣。我們眾生，就譬如方才所說那個蒙上眼睛的人，這個人本來沒有盲，只不過受一塊布帛的遮掩。眾生也是如此，我們的心性，本來也沒有失掉，本來也

easy? Skeptical and dull living beings might ask that. But the Bodhisattvas are determined to give living beings a bargain, which is the reason they spoke this expedient Dharma-door. Nevertheless, some living beings are still unaware of this supreme bargain. What a pity!

Some people say, "I believe that reciting the Bodhisattva's name can dissolve offenses and eradicate suffering, but how can it cause us to understand the mind and see the nature?" A few days ago I used the analogy of making phone calls. Now I will give a simpler analogy.

Suppose a person is blindfolded so that he only sees total darkness. When he tries to walk, he keeps bumping into the walls until he's bruised and terribly sore. However, it doesn't occur to him to take off the blindfold. Luckily, he meets a kind person who sees his miserable state and removes the blindfold for him. Now he can see, and he won't hurt himself by bumping into the walls anymore.

The same principle holds in reciting the Bodhisattva's name. We living beings are like the blindfolded person. He isn't really blind; his eyes are merely covered by a piece of cloth. Likewise, we living beings haven't lost our mind and nature. They are originally clear and bright, but they have been covered over by countless obstructions from offenses and idle thoughts. The Bodhisattva is like the kind person, for he removes the karmic obstructions covering our inherent bright nature, allowing us to return to the source and regain our original face.

是磊落光明，只是被無數的罪障、妄念遮蔽罷了。菩薩，譬如那位慈悲的人，他替我們解除那些掩蔽著我們光明本性的業障；於是，我們便可以返本還原，恢復到本來的面目了。

所以，我們不可不念菩薩的名號，就像那個被蒙上眼睛的人，若是不肯求援，也不肯接受別人的幫助，那麼碰壁事小，可是若因為看不見路途而掉進深淵，那豈不是危害了自己的性命！

世界上誘人的罪惡多得很，若是一不小心，掉進了罪惡的深淵，失掉了人身，那便是萬劫不復，千古遺恨了。居士們！趕快接受菩薩的勸諭，常常持誦菩薩的洪名，讓菩薩快些救度我們脫離這生死的苦海吧！

一九五八年六月十七日下午開示

We cannot fail to recite the Bodhisattva's name, or it would be like the blind man refusing to be helped by others. Bumping into the wall is a small matter, but if he can't see where he's going and he walks into an abyss, his life is certainly in danger.

There are plenty of offenses which we may be tempted to commit in this world, and if we are not careful, we could fall into the abyss of offenses and lose our human body. We may not return for ten thousand eons, and we will regret it for ages. Laypeople! Quickly accept the Bodhisattva's exhortations and recite the Bodhisattva's great name constantly, so the Bodhisattva can soon save us from the bitter sea of birth and death!

A talk given on the afternoon of June 17, 1958

眾生無邊誓願度

我們能忍心讓他們痛苦，
不設法令他們快樂嗎？

菩薩畏因，眾生畏果，因、果這兩個字，不但我
們眾生逃不了，甚至於連佛、菩薩也不能避免的
，只因菩薩的眼光遠大，所以不造惡因，而受的
也是樂果，可是眾生卻眼光如豆，只爲目前打算
，常種惡因，所以也常吃苦果。

所謂「多栽桃李少栽荊」。多種善因，無疑地就
是替自己預備了錦繡的前程，假若只顧目前，多
行不義，不種善因，那麼無疑地也是替自己的前
途預備了荊棘的途徑。

什麼是錦繡前程呢？「遙指西方落日邊」，「從
是西方。過十萬億佛土。有世界名曰極樂。」

什麼是荊棘前程呢？啊！「地獄無門苦自招」，

Living Beings Are Boundless; I Vow to Save Them All.

How can we bear to let them suffer, and not find a way to bring them happiness?

Bodhisattvas fear causes; living beings fear effects. It is not only living beings who cannot escape cause and effect; even the Buddhas and Bodhisattvas cannot avoid them. However, because Bodhisattvas have far-ranging vision, they avoid creating bad causes and only receive joyful rewards. Living beings, on the other hand, are very short-sighted. Seeing only what's in front of them, they often plant evil causes, and so they must often suffer the bitter retribution.

It is said, "Plant more peach and plum trees, and fewer thorn bushes." By planting more good causes, you will undoubtedly be laying out a golden future for yourself. But if you only see the present, and you engage in lots of immoral practices and plant no good causes, you will doubtlessly be preparing a thorny path to travel in the future.

What is the golden future? "Point to the distant setting sun in the West." "To the west of here, passing a hundred thousand million Buddha-lands, is a land called Ultimate Bliss."

What is the thorny future? "Hell has no gates; you bring suffering

在極樂世界裏，黃金爲地，七寶爲池，天樂風飄處處聞，事事無不稱心滿意，還可以見聞佛法，速成佛道；然而在地獄裏呢？刀山、油鑊、劍樹、洪爐，就是最好的伴侶了。

對於選擇前程，眾生是絕對自由的。若是志在西方，發願要往生淨土的話，那麼要精勤念佛菩薩的名號便可以了；若是歡喜地獄，更簡單，行惡事就墮地獄，這是必然的。可是我敢肯定地說一句，沒有人寧願下地獄，而不願往生西方極樂世界的。除非他不信有地獄和有極樂，除非他不知道有痛苦的地獄和極樂的淨土。

對於「斷善根、少信心」的人，我們是沒有辦法度的；可是對於「不知道」的人，我們卻應該生出一種慈悲的心。外道的人常說：「天國近了，天國是你們的」。我們信佛的人，也應該爲法忘軀，奔走跋涉，對自己的親友們，說說念菩薩的功德，和極樂世界的好處。「極樂世界是眾生的」，若是你能常常說這種道理，那麼你就是一個大道心的菩薩了，和菩薩一樣行徑的人，就是不退菩薩爲伴侶了。

upon yourself." In the Land of Ultimate Bliss, the ground is made of gold and the pools are filled with the seven gems. Celestial music is carried by the breeze and heard everywhere, and everything goes according to your wishes. You can also see the Buddha, hear the Dharma, and quickly accomplish Buddhahood. What about the hells? Your best companions there are the Mountain of Knives, the Oil Cauldron, the Tree of Swords, and the Great Furnace.

Living beings are absolutely free to choose their own future. If you wish to be born in the West and you make a vow to that effect, you can accomplish it by vigorously reciting the names of the Buddhas and Bodhisattvas. If you prefer the hells, it's even easier—just do evil deeds and you'll fall into the hells for sure. But I can assure you of one thing: no one would prefer falling into the hells to being reborn in the Land of Ultimate Bliss. That is, unless he doesn't believe in the hells and the Land of Ultimate Bliss, or he doesn't know that the hells are misery and the Pure Land is blissful.

If people have cut off their good roots or have little faith, there is no way for us to save them. But if it's a matter of not knowing, we should be compassionate. Other religions often say, "The Kingdom of Heaven is near. The Kingdom of Heaven belongs to you." We of the Buddhist faith should also forget our bodies for the sake of the Dharma, and hasten to tell our friends and relatives about the merit and virtue of reciting the Bodhisattva's name, and the benefits of the Land of Ultimate Bliss. "The Land of Ultimate Bliss belongs to living beings." If you constantly proclaim this kind of principle, you are truly a Bodhisattva with a great mind for the Way. Those who walk the same path as the Bodhisattvas will have irreversible Bodhisattvas as their companions.

所以，我們不但自己要念菩薩，也應常常勸別人也念菩薩，這樣，才可以說得上是一個佛教徒，才可以說是不忘皈依時所發的四宏誓願，所謂「獨樂樂，不如眾樂樂」。一切眾生，皆有佛性，對於具有相同佛性，與自己無分別的眾生，我們能忍心讓他們痛苦，不設法令他們快樂嗎？

「有志者，事竟成」，眾生雖然難度，可是我們信佛的人，二六時中，切記不要忘了度眾生。

一九五八年六月十八日上午開示

Therefore, we should recite the Bodhisattva's name ourselves, and frequently urge others to recite it as well. Then we can be considered Buddhist disciples, and we can say we haven't forgotten the Four Vast Vows we made when we took refuge. It's said, "Solitary happiness is not as good as happiness shared with everyone." Since all living beings have the same Buddha-nature and are no different from us in that respect, how can we bear to let them suffer, and not find a way to bring them happiness?

"Where there's a will, there's a way." Although living beings are hard to save, we who are Buddhists must never forget to save living beings.

A talk given on the morning of June 18, 1958

學佛要修戒定慧

常常拿「戒定慧」來警惕自己，
這對於修行是會有所幫助的。

戒、定、慧三無漏學，是修行人所必須具有的。

戒，雖然有五戒、十戒、菩薩戒等等，然而最基本的，要算是五戒，那就是戒殺、戒盜、戒邪淫、戒妄語和戒飲酒。能持戒，就不會造罪。

什麼是「定」呢？照普通來說，就是禪定。範圍廣一點來說，就是不變的意思。有些人修行，妄想很多，今天參禪，明天聽說念佛的功德大，於是便捨參禪而念佛，過兩天又聽說念咒的功德殊勝，於是又不念佛而念咒，諸如此類。今天修這個法門，明天又修那個法門，結果一事無成。又有些人對於念佛和念菩薩，一曝十寒，今天念，明天便不念，這都是沒有定力的緣故。定力對於我們修行，是非常重要的，如果沒有定力，那麼

To Study Buddhism, We Must Cultivate Precepts, Samadhi, and Wisdom

Always use precepts, samadhi, and wisdom to alert yourself; this will help you in your cultivation.

Every cultivator needs to have the Three Non-Outflow Studies of precepts, samadhi, and wisdom.

Precepts: Although there are the Five Precepts, the Ten Precepts, the Bodhisattva Precepts, and so on, the Five Precepts are the most fundamental. They are: do not kill, do not steal, do not engage in sexual misconduct, do not engage in false speech, and do not take intoxicants. If one can hold the precepts, one will not make transgressions.

What is samadhi? Ordinarily, samadhi refers to Dhyana (Chan) samadhi. Generally speaking, it means "unchanging." When some people cultivate, they do a lot of idle thinking. Today they practice Chan meditation, but tomorrow they hear that reciting the Buddha's name has a lot of merit and virtue, so they give up Chan and go recite the Buddha's name. Two days later they hear the merit and virtue of reciting mantras is supreme, so they stop reciting the Buddha's name and start reciting mantras instead. In general, that's how they carry on. Cultivating this Dharma-door today and that Dharma-door tomorrow, they end up achieving nothing. There are also some people who recite the Buddha's or Bodhisattva's name

，修道一定不成，而且也會因爲缺乏定力、道心
不堅的緣故，很容易受到外來的引誘而墮落。

其次，說到「慧」，就是智慧。世界上的人，有
賢愚之分，究竟爲什麼有些人聰明，而有些人卻
愚癡？當然有其中的因果，凡是在過去生中修行
念佛的人，今生較有智慧，反之，不曾種下善根
的，智慧便遜人一籌了。

《大學》裏說：

> 定而後能靜，
> 靜而後能安，
> 安而後能慮，
> 慮而後能得。

所以由「定」中，也可以產生出「慧」，若是不
「定」的話，那麼雜念叢生，奔波勞碌，又怎能
冷靜地判別是非、明白眞理呢？

「戒」，是一種規律，防止我們犯罪的；在不犯
罪中，我們又要修道。而修道的祕訣是「定力」

with the attitude of "sunning it one day and freezing it for ten." They recite today, but quit tomorrow. This is because they have no samadhi. Samadhi is extremely important in our cultivation. If we have no samadhi, we will surely have no success in cultivation. Moreover, if we do not have sufficient samadhi and we lack a firm resolve in the Way, external temptations can easily influence us and cause us to fall.

Next there is "wisdom." In the world, there are wise people and stupid people. Why is it that some people are smart and some are stupid? Of course, it involves cause and effect. All those who cultivated by reciting the Buddha's name in former lives have comparatively more wisdom in this life. But those who didn't plant good roots in the past have less wisdom than most people.

The Great Learning says,

> *When a person has concentration, he can be still.*
> *When he is still, he can be at peace.*
> *When he is at peace, he can reflect.*
> *Upon reflection, he can obtain what he wants.*

If you are in samadhi, you can produce wisdom. But if you are not concentrated, if you produce droves of scattered thoughts, if you are hasty and flighty, then how can you calmly distinguish right from wrong and understand the truth?

Precepts are rules which keep us from committing offenses. While refraining from committing offenses, we should also cultivate the Way, and the secret to cultivating the Way is samadhi power. Once

。有了定力，便能產生智慧，更能進一步地了道，成佛。所以，「戒定慧」這三個字，是修行人所必須具有的條件。不持戒，就會造罪招業；缺乏定力，就會修道不成；沒有智慧，便會愚癡無知。

我勸在座各位，都能把「戒定慧」這三個字，作爲修道的座右銘，常常拿來警惕自己，那麼，我相信對於修行，是會有點幫助的。

一九五八年六月十八日下午開示

you have samadhi power, you can develop wisdom, and if you can progress one step further, you can understand the Way and become a Buddha. That is why the three studies of precepts, samadhi, and wisdom are the essential requirements which all people who cultivate the Way should possess. If you do not hold the precepts, then you can create offenses and call forth karma. Lacking samadhi power, you will not be able to accomplish cultivation of the Way. You will not have any wisdom and will become dull-witted.

I exhort you all to take special note of the three studies of precepts, samadhi, and wisdom in your cultivation; always use them to alert yourself and I believe it will help you in your cultivation.

A talk given on the afternoon of June 18, 1958

寺前湧出常流水

這裏本來沒有水的，卻變成有水，
難道真是我把水搬來的嗎？

今天是菩薩聖誕，西樂園雖然建在三百多級的山上，可是來到這裏參加打七的人，卻非常踴躍，這足見凡是來參加賀誕的人，個個都是具有真心，而且又是勇猛精進的。

從人數來說，這八年來參加打七的人一年比一年多，而且，更有很多人來這裏拜佛後說自己一切都比從前順利。

譬如：袁果林居士，自從來西樂園以後，生意特別興旺。譚果璞居士，皈依後也能增福延壽，今年八十多歲了，可是身體仍然非常健康。

又有一個腿不方便，從四歲起，到九歲都不能走路，可是在這裏拜佛後，就能走路了。此外，李

A Constantly Bubbling Spring Appeared by the Temple

This place originally had no water, but now it does. Is it possible that I really brought the water with me?

Today is the Bodhisattva's birthday, and although this temple is built three hundred steps up the mountain, all you who have come to this session have proved to be very nimble. Thus, each person who has come to celebrate the birthday is not only true-hearted, but courageous and vigorous as well.

I've taken note of the number of people who have attended these sessions over the past eight years, and every year the attendance is larger. And more and more people who come to bow and pay their respects during the session have said they found afterwards that everything went more smoothly for them.

For example, Upasika Yuan Guolin said that since she started coming to Western Bliss Garden Monastery, her business has been especially prosperous. And ever since Upasaka Tan Guopu took refuge, his blessings have increased and his life has been lengthened, so that although he is over eighty, he is still in excellent health.

There is also the crippled child who had been lame since the age of four. At age nine he started coming here to bow to the Buddha, and now he can walk. Then there is Li Guoyuan's daughter, who broke

果遠居士的女兒腿跌壞了，中西醫和跌打醫生都不能治好，也是拜佛後就好了。所以有人就謠傳我會治病，其實這不過是拜佛的功德罷了。

還有一件事，可以作為紀念的：就是在西樂園未建成以前，原屬一個七、八尺深的大坑，經過了人工、泥工的填平之後，才能建立這個道場。而且這裏從前是沒有水的，可是在道場建成之後，就有一股水源源不絕而至。有人說，這股水是我從芙蓉山帶來的；因為我在觀音洞住的時候，洞前有水，可是說也奇怪，自從我搬到西樂園後，觀音洞這個水就沒有了。而這裏本來沒有水的，卻變成有水，難道真是我把水搬來的嗎？這一切無非都是佛、菩薩的感應，龍天的擁護。

今天，大家都是這麼高興、這麼踴躍，然而盛會不常，又要到明年才舉行了。明年打觀音七，大家請早。而且，更要發願打個全七，還有在十一月的阿彌陀佛七，大家也要勇猛精進，切勿放逸懈怠。

現在，我有一個無上的法門，想說給大家聽，可

her leg so badly that neither Chinese nor Western specialists could set it for her. After she started bowing to the Buddhas here, her leg healed. Because of such incidents, some people have spread the rumor that I can cure illnesses. Actually, it's just the merit and virtue of bowing to the Buddhas.

There is another incident of note. Before Western Bliss Garden Monastery was constructed, this was just a barren plot of land marred by a pit seven or eight feet deep. Much labor was spent filling in the pit with mud and then levelling off the ground before the Bodhimanda could be built. Besides that, there had never been any water here, but after the Bodhimanda was built, an unending supply of water appeared. Some people say I brought the water with me from Furung Mountain. That's because while I lived there in Guanyin Cave, there was water in front of the cave, but strange as it may sound, after I moved to Western Bliss Garden, the water disappeared. And this place, which originally had no water, now has water. Is it possible that I really brought the water with me? This whole situation is nothing more than a response from the Buddhas, Bodhisattvas, and the protective dragons and gods.

Today everyone is happy and enthusiastic, but the session is almost over, and we must wait until next year to hold another one. Everyone who plans to attend next year's Guanyin Recitation Session should sign up early, and moreover, you should make a vow to attend the entire session. In the eleventh lunar month there will be an Amitabha Buddha Recitation Session, and those who attend should be courageously vigorous and not the least bit lazy or lax.

I now have an unsurpassed Dharma-door that I intend to speak for

是在未說之前，我得告訴大家，求法並不容易，
所以大家先要答應我，在聽後依法修行，我才能
說。

這個法門，就是每天在佛前發願：

> 眾生無邊誓願度，
> 煩惱無盡誓願斷，
> 法門無量誓願學，
> 佛道無上誓願成。

這是大家都知道的，而且諸佛也都是從此而成，
菩薩也是從此而修。還有一個大家更熟悉的，就
是：

> 願生西方淨土中，
> 九品蓮華爲父母；
> 花開見佛悟無生，
> 不退菩薩爲伴侶。

大家若能每天都這樣發願，那麼，我可以保證大
家定能面見慈尊，獲不退轉，早成佛道的。

一九五八年六月十九日上午開示

you, but before I tell it to you, I should remind you that seeking the Dharma is not an easy matter. Therefore all of you should first agree to rely on the Dharma to cultivate, and then I will explain this unsurpassed dharma to you.

The Dharma-door consists of making vows before the Buddhas every single day. Vow:

> *Living beings are boundless; I vow to save them.*
> *Afflictions are endless; I vow to cut them off.*
> *Dharma-doors are limitless; I vow to study them all.*
> *The Buddha Way is unsurpassed; I vow to realize it.*

These vows are familiar to everyone. What is more, they are the means by which all Buddhas attained realization, and they are the vows that all Bodhisattvas cultivate. There is another vow with which everyone is even more familiar:

> *I vow to be reborn in the Pure Land*
> *With the nine grades of lotuses as my father*
> *   and mother.*
> *When the flower opens I will see the Buddha*
> *   and awaken to the unproduced.*
> *Irreversible Bodhisattvas will befriend me.*

If everyone can make these vows every single day, I can guarantee that each of you will be able to meet the Compassionate Honored One, obtain irreversibility, and soon realize the Buddha Way.

A talk given on the morning of June 19, 1958

金山聖寺的家風

從早晨兩點鐘開始坐香，一直到夜間
十二點睡覺，中間只有一個鐘頭休息。

今逢一九七六年，十方大眾來參禪；
時刻分秒當愛惜，行住坐臥細鑽研。
虛空打破明心地，法界依然見性天；
本來面目何處見，直下承當金山寺。

今天是一九七六年十二月十五日，十方有善根的
人，來到金山聖寺這個大冶洪爐參禪。參禪不是
很好玩的一件事，要受很多苦。從早晨兩點鐘開
始坐香，一直到夜間十二點睡覺，中間只有一個
鐘頭休息，這是金山聖寺的家風。

在參禪的期間，要忘身、忘心、忘世，一切皆忘
掉，也就是沒有「我」的存在，也就是一切皆空
，到了真空的境界，便生妙有。大家要注意！在
休息的時間，不可以隨便亂講話，不可以隨便打
妄想，更不可躲懶偷安，就是一分一秒的時間，

The Tradition at Gold Mountain Monastery

Meditation starts at 2 A.M. and goes until midnight, at which time people can sleep. During the day there is only one hour of rest.

Now we come to the year of 1976.
The multitudes gather from the ten directions to investigate Chan.
Every hour, minute, and second must be cherished.
While walking, standing, sitting, and lying down,
Investigate deeply and carefully.
Empty space is shattered, and you understand the Mind's Ground.
The Dharma Realm remains the same, yet you see the Nature's Sky.
Where can you find your original face?
Right here at Gold Mountain Monastery!

Today is December 15, 1976, and people endowed with good roots have come from the ten directions to the great smelting furnace (Gold Mountain Monastery) to investigate Chan. Investigating Chan is not a very fun affair; you must take a lot of suffering. Meditation starts at 2 A.M. and goes until midnight, at which time people can sleep. During the day there is only one hour of rest. That's the traditional practice at the Gold Mountain Monastery.

During the Chan session, you must forget the body, the mind, and the world. You must forget everything, which means you must have no "self" and see everything as empty. When you reach the state of true emptiness, wonderful existence comes forth. Everyone, pay attention! In cultivation, you must not chatter casually or have

也要愛惜，所謂：

> 一寸時光，一寸命光。

所以，行也參禪，住也參禪，坐也參禪，臥也參禪，行住坐臥都在參禪，要細心來鑽研，越鑽越透、越研越明。

鑽研，就是參話頭。不要停止，時時刻刻來參「念佛是誰？」或參「父母未生以前的本來面目？」所以要細鑽研。有一天把虛空打破，這個時候，就能明白心。虛空雖然破了，可是法界依然存在。法界還是十法界，井然不亂。這時候，見到自己的性天。你們的本來面目，要到什麼地方去尋找呢？你們到金山聖寺來找本來面目，到旁的地方是找不到的。

這是今天所說的八句偈頌，希望各位留心記住，依法修行，不可當飯把它吃掉，食而不化，這是無有是處；不可當作耳邊風，過而不留，聽了等於沒有聽一樣無用。

一九七六年禪七　十二月十五日開示於三藩市金山聖寺

random thoughts. Even less should you be lazy and try to take it easy. Every minute and second must be cherished. It is said,

An inch of time is an inch of life.

Therefore, you should be investigating Chan while you are walking, standing, sitting, and lying down. In all of these modes, you should be investigating Chan. Your investigation should be penetrating and thorough, so that the deeper you go, the more you understand, and the more you look into it, the clearer you become.

This refers to investigating the meditation topic. Don't ever stop. Constantly investigate "Who is mindful of the Buddha?" or "What was my original face before my parents gave birth to me?" You must enter deeply and investigate in detail. One day, you will be able to shatter empty space, and at that time you will understand the mind. Even though empty space is shattered, the Dharma Realm remains intact. The ten Dharma Realms are still in order and not mixed up. At that point you will see your own nature, which is like the sky. Where can you go to search for your original face? You can come to Gold Mountain Monastery to look for it. If you go elsewhere, you won't find it.

This is an explanation of the eight lines of verse I spoke today. I hope each of you will remember it well, and cultivate according to it. Don't just swallow it without digesting it. That would be useless. Don't let it just go in one ear and out the other, without retaining any impression. That would be as useless as not hearing it at all.

A talk given on December 15, 1976, during a
Chan Session at Gold Mountain Monastery in San Francisco

學佛法要拿出眞心

一舉一動，一言一行
都要往眞的做。

學佛法要拿出眞心，一舉一動，一言一行都要往眞的做。不像世間人，半眞半假，有時說點眞話，有時說點假話。修道人時時要講眞話，做眞事，不打妄語。每一念都要除我們自己的毛病，自己往昔無量劫習氣都要改掉，無量劫以來的罪業都要懺悔。

爲什麼學佛法學得很久，卻都沒有相應呢？就因爲保護著我們的過錯，不肯拿出眞心修行，所以把光陰都空過，也沒有開眞正智慧，也沒得眞正的定力。時間空過，自己道業也沒成就，這是很可惜的一件事。

在道場裏，要節省一切物質，所謂：

愛惜常住物，
如護眼中珠。

In Studying Buddhism, You Must Use a True Mind

In every move you make and every word you say, you should aim to be true.

In studying Buddhism, you must bring forth a true mind. In every move you make and every word you say, you should aim to be true. Don't be like worldly people, half true and half false, sometimes telling the truth and sometimes telling lies. Cultivators must always speak truthfully, do true deeds, and not tell lies. In every thought, we must get rid of our own faults. We must correct the bad habits we have formed since limitless eons in the past and repent of the offenses created in limitless eons.

Why haven't we had any response after studying the Buddhadharma for so long? It's because we have defended our own faults and have not brought forth a true resolve to cultivate. Therefore, we have wasted all this time and have not achieved any real wisdom or attained any real samadhi. The time has passed in vain, and we have not had any accomplishment in our cultivation. This is very lamentable.

In the monastery, we must be thrifty with all materials. It is said,

> *Cherish the things of the temple*
> *As if they were the pupils in your own eyes.*

「常住物」，譬如所吃的米、油、醬、醋，要愛惜，不要糟蹋，不要浪費。所用的甚至一根草，一塊木頭，一張紙都要愛惜保護；在這上面若不小心，不知惜福，就把功德都漏掉了。

> 所修的，不如所造的；
> 所得的，不如所丟的。

再者，一舉一動，一言一行都不要傷害到其他的人，口上也要存德，不說綺語、妄語、惡口、兩舌，口德特別要注意；身不殺生、不偷盜、不邪淫；意念裏不犯貪、瞋、癡，不要盡為這臭皮囊著想，心心念念要為它偷東西吃，心心念念想要把這臭皮囊裝飾得好看一點，心心念念想叫這臭皮囊享受一點，快樂一點，這都是顛倒。我們若想出離三界，脫離六道輪迴，都要把這習氣改掉。情愛也要把它看空了，才能遂心滿願，成就你的菩提道果。

「修道不能享福」，要記得佛教的老祖宗——釋迦牟尼佛當初修道時，貴為太子，富可敵國，他能毅然出家修道。以他的身分來說，雖然出家仍

The things of the temple include the rice, oil, sauce, and vinegar that we consume. We should cherish them and not let them spoil and go to waste. We should cherish and take care of even a blade of grass, a piece of wood, or a sheet of paper that we use. If we are not careful in this and do not cherish our blessings, all our merit and virtue will leak out. Then,

> *Our offenses will exceed our blessings, and*
> *Our losses will surpass our gains.*

Moreover, in our every move and every word, we must not hurt anyone else. We should guard the virtue of our mouth, not speaking frivolous words, untruthful words, harsh words, or words which cause disharmony. We should pay special attention to the virtue of our mouth. With our body, we should not kill, steal, or be promiscuous. In our mind, we should not have greed, hatred, or stupidity. We shouldn't always be worrying about our stinking skinbag, finding good things to feed it in every thought, trying to make it more attractive in every thought. In thought after thought, you only want the stinking skinbag to enjoy more pleasure—that's upside down. If we want to escape the Triple Realm and leave the six paths of rebirth, we must get rid of all these bad habits. We must also see through love and emotion. Only then can we fulfill our vows and accomplish the fruition of Bodhi.

In cultivation, we cannot enjoy our blessings. We must remember that when Shakyamuni Buddha, the founder of Buddhism, started cultivating, he was a noble prince of tremendous wealth. Nevertheless, he resolutely left the home-life to cultivate the Way. Given his status, even after he left home he could have eaten well,

然可吃好的，穿好的，住一座好房子，可是他沒有這樣做，他跑到雪山那裏，忍苦、忍餓、忍寒、忍熱，在那兒修行了六年，在這六年之間沒有吃過什麼好的東西，也沒有各處去叫人供養他，就是在那兒受苦。

以釋迦牟尼佛那種富貴的身分，尚且自己願意受苦來修行，我們又是什麼身分呢？不過是很普通平凡的人，為什麼要穿好、吃好、住好，貪圖享受，受不了苦，怕受苦？想想，比起釋迦牟尼佛，我們是不是要生大慚愧？

dressed well, and lived in a fine house, but he didn't. He went to the Himalayas and cultivated for six years, enduring pain, hunger, cold and heat. During those six years, he never ate any good food or went around asking people to make offerings to him. He just endured the suffering.

Even with his position of wealth and honor, Shakyamuni Buddha was willing to suffer and cultivate. What is our position? We are just ordinary, common people, yet why do we still want to dress well, eat well, live well, and enjoy ourselves? Why can't we take suffering? Why do we fear suffering? Think about it. When we compare ourselves to Shakyamuni Buddha, shouldn't we feel great remorse?

應無所住而生其心

你要行所無事，做出來了，
還要不執著你有什麼功德。

作禮無住化往生，
無窮無盡義彌豐；
十方如來同攝受，
離苦得樂出火坑。

在佛教裏常言：「應無所住而生其心」。所以我
在講〈楞嚴咒〉不是說：「作禮無住化往生」，
這個「生」就是生生無定、化化無窮的意思。作
禮，就是向佛頂禮。無所住，就是叫你沒有執著
；你說那麼我不要修行就沒有執著，這就錯了。
你修行也不要執著有修行。你說那麼我不吃飯時
，不去執著沒有吃飯，可是肚子卻不答應。可是
你吃飽了，還想要再吃，那也是不對的。《金剛
經》上說：「應無所住而生其心。」

今天有一個人，以為這個「應無所住而生其心」

112

You Should Produce the Thought Which Abides Nowhere

You have to do things as if not doing them. After you've done something, don't be attached to the merit and virtue that you've created.

> *Pay homage while abiding nowhere, and*
> *transform beings to go to rebirth.*
> *Endless and inexhaustible, the meanings are prolific.*
> *The Tathagatas of the ten directions together*
> *gather us in,*
> *So that we can leave suffering, attain bliss,*
> *and escape the pit of fire.*

In Buddhism, we often say, "One should produce the thought which abides nowhere." And so, in explaining the Shurangama Mantra, I said, "Pay homage while abiding nowhere, and transform beings to go to rebirth." Rebirth refers to undergoing indefinite births and endless transformations. "Paying homage" refers to bowing to the Buddhas. "Abiding nowhere" means you should have no attachments. You say, "Well, I won't cultivate, and then I won't have any attachments." That's wrong. Although you cultivate, you should not be attached to the notion that you are cultivating. You say, "If I don't eat and I don't attach to the fact that I have not eaten, my stomach won't agree with me." However, if you've eaten your fill and you want to eat more, that's also wrong. The *Vajra Sutra* says, "You should produce the thought which abides nowhere."

，就是不要修行，不要念咒，也不要念經，那就沒有執著了。不是的，你要「行所無事」，做出來了，還要不執著你有什麼功德，這叫無所住。因為你有所住，就會黏到那個地方飛不動，所以要無住身心，掃一切法，離一切相，生生化化，無窮無盡，所以說：「無窮無盡義彌豐」，這一句咒文的義理是無窮無盡的，意義是多得不得了，再也沒有那麼多了。

因為這樣，所以你一念這句咒，「十方如來同攝受」，十方諸佛都攝受你，就像哄小孩子似的，說：「你不要哭了，我有糖給你吃；不要哭了，等一等我送你兩個蘋果。」小孩子一聽到蘋果，耳朵就伸出來了，舌頭在嘴裏也裝不住了。就是這樣，十方如來同攝受你，令你「離苦得樂出火坑」。

Today someone thought the words, "You should produce the thought which abides nowhere," meant that if you didn't cultivate, recite mantras, or recite Sutras, you would be without attachments. That's not it. What you have to do is do things as if not doing them. After you've done something, don't be attached to the merit and virtue that you've created. That's called "abiding nowhere." If you abide somewhere, you will get stuck in one place and be unable to get out. So you must not dwell on the body or mind; sweep away all dharmas and separate from all appearances. Then the process of creation and transformation will be endless and inexhaustible. So the next sentence says, "Endless and inexhaustible, the meanings are prolific." The meanings of this mantra are endless and inexhaustible. It has an incredible amount of meaning; nothing else has that much meaning.

Therefore, when you recite this mantra, "The Tathagatas of the ten directions together gather us in." The Buddhas of the ten directions all draw you in, treating you like a child, saying, "Don't cry anymore. I'll give you some candy to eat. Don't cry. Wait a bit, and I'll give you a couple of apples." Hearing the word "apples," the child's ears perk up and he licks his lips in anticipation. In that way, the Tathagatas of the ten directions gather you in, enabling you to "leave suffering, attain bliss, and escape the pit of fire."

「無漏」的智慧光明

若是有了欲念，好像常被土匪打劫，
財寶被搶去了。

諸佛菩薩、賢聖僧，皆有無上的大智光明，無漏
無盡的智慧。

人有漏，因為有「無明」；佛菩薩無漏，因為無
「無明」。無明，就是無所明了，也就是糊塗，
不明是非，不辨黑白。

最大的漏，就是欲漏。若是有了欲念，好像常被
土匪打劫，財寶被搶去了；好像木材內生蟲子，
沒有用處了；又好像在美食中放了糞便一樣，令
人作嘔三日。

有人說：「人人都有欲念嘛！」就因為這個緣故
，所以才要修行，要教他沒有欲念，才能現出本
來的智慧光明。所以「無漏」，是修行人所求之
瑰寶。

The Wisdom Light of "Non-outflows"

If you have thoughts of desire, it's as if your wealth and treasures are always getting plundered by bandits.

All the Buddhas, Bodhisattvas, Worthy Ones and Sages of the Sangha have a great wisdom light which is unsurpassed. Their wisdom is free of outflows and inexhaustible.

People have outflows because they have ignorance. Buddhas and Bodhisattvas have no outflows, because they have no ignorance. Being ignorant means not understanding anything. It means being muddled, and not being able to tell right from wrong, or black from white.

The biggest outflow is the outflow of desire. If you have thoughts of desire, it's as if your wealth and treasures are always getting plundered by bandits. It's like wood which becomes infested with termites, making it useless. It's also like delicious food to which manure is added, making people throw up for three days.

Someone says, "But everyone has thoughts of desire!" That's exactly the reason we must cultivate. We have to get rid of thoughts of desire before our inherent wisdom can come forth. Thus, the state of "non-outflows" is the extraordinary treasure sought by cultivators.

117

各位！要特別注意。在六神通中，為什麼有「漏盡通」？就是沒有漏的意思，也就是完全沒有欲念。所謂「斷欲去愛」，人能修到爐火純青的時候，就得到自在。若是不斷欲、不去愛，常被無明支配，令你顛倒行事，一天到晚不自在、不舒服，這就是欲念在作怪。

各位善知識！在這個地方要特別用一番功夫，返本還原，恢復本來面目，這個時候，就得到無盡的智慧，源源而來，取之不盡，用之不竭。

各位要發菩提心，才能打破生死關。自己要反省，撫心自問：為什麼要信佛？為什麼要出家？為什麼出家不修行？為什麼出家之後，還要打那麼多的妄想？這些問題不要放過，若把它們想通了，就能出離三界，了生脫死，得到涅槃的快樂。

Everyone should pay close attention. Why is the spiritual power of Elimination of Outflows one of the six spiritual powers? Elimination of Outflows means to have no outflows and to be totally free of desire, as in the saying, "Cut off desire and cast out love." If you can cultivate until you attain mastery, you will experience a sense of freedom and ease. But if you don't put an end to love and desire, and are always controlled by ignorance, you will do upside-down things and be ill at ease all day long, because your thoughts of desire are acting up.

All Good and Wise Advisors! You should especially apply effort in this, return to the source, recover your original face—at that point, you will attain an inexhaustible wisdom which comes forth incessantly. No matter how much you use, it will never be exhausted.

Each of you must bring forth the resolve for Bodhi—only then can you smash through the gate of birth and death. You must look within yourself and ask your conscience: Why do I believe in the Buddha? Why did I leave the home-life? Why don't I cultivate after leaving home? Having left home, why do I still have so many idle thoughts? Don't bypass these questions. You should think them through clearly! Then you'll be able to leave the Triple Realm, end birth and death, and attain the bliss of Nirvana.

修德、造業

終日在醉生夢死中度生活，
一點功德也沒有修，怎能成佛？

各位想一想，佛在往昔修無量無邊的功德，才能
成佛。

我們為什麼沒有成佛？就因為沒有修無量無邊的
功德。我們的功德相差太遠，因為一邊修行，一
邊造業，所謂「修的沒有造的多」。

一天到晚造身業、造口業、造意業。譬如，在意
念裏，常想人家不好，想著人家對不起我，想人
家不如我等等妄想，於是在意念中，造了很多貪
瞋癡的罪業。在口上也造業，講是說非，盡打妄
語、綺語、惡口、兩舌等等。有些人要是一天不
講是講非，就好像一天不能活著；一天不打妄想
，就好像沒有吃飯一樣不自在。一天到晚，要靠
講是非、打妄想來生存，你們說怪不怪？真令人
費解。

Cultivating Virtue versus Creating Karma

If you spend your whole life in a muddle, born drunk and dying in a dream, and not cultivating the least bit of merit and virtue, how can you become a Buddha?

Each of you should think for a moment: in the past, the Buddha had to cultivate limitless and boundless merit and virtue before he could become a Buddha.

Why haven't we become Buddhas? It's because we haven't cultivated limitless and boundless merit and virtue. Our merit and virtue are far less, because we cultivate on one hand and create karma on the other. So it is said, "What we cultivate is not as much as what we create."

From morning to night, we create karma with our body, with our mouth, and with our mind. For example, in our thoughts, we often have idle thoughts about how bad people are, how others have wronged us, how others are not as good as we are, and so forth. As a result, we create a lot of evil karma with the greed, anger and stupidity in our thoughts. We also create karma with our mouth, always talking about others' rights and wrongs, constantly telling lies, saying indecent things, scolding people, backbiting, and so on. There are some people who don't seem to be able to survive for even a day without gossiping. If they don't tell lies for a day, they feel as uncomfortable as if they hadn't eaten. All day long, they

有這種毛病的人，自己還不承認，還要瞞著遮蓋它，還說自己沒有打妄想，沒有欲念，戴著假面具，到處騙人。其實在這世界上，怎能騙得了人？不但騙不了人，連自己也騙不了。為什麼？因為自己打妄想，問問自己知道不知道？若是知道，那就騙不了自己，既然騙不了自己，怎能騙人呢？愚癡人才有這種的行為。

不修行的人，戴著假面具，昧心厚顏，專做些不守規矩、不光明正大的事，自己還不承認。因之，終日在醉生夢死中度生活，一點功德也沒有修，怎能成佛？與佛相差十萬八千里。

換句話說，我們所修的功德，還沒有造的孽業多；也可以說：「所得的沒有所丟的多。」這樣焉能有所成就？

need to gossip and lie in order to survive. Wouldn't you say that's strange? It really hard to figure them out.

Yet the people who have this fault still refuse to admit it. They still want to cover it up, and they claim they haven't told any lies and don't have any desires. They put on a mask and cheat everyone. Actually, in this world, how can you succeed in cheating people? Not only can you not cheat others, you can't even cheat yourself. Why not? When you have idle thoughts, ask yourself if you are aware of them. If you are aware of them, that means you can't fool yourself. Since you can't cheat yourself, how can you cheat others? Only stupid people behave that way.

People who don't cultivate will put on a mask and in blind shamelessness do a lot of devious, improper deeds that break the rules. Yet they won't admit it. Because of this, they spend their whole life in a muddle, born drunk and dying in a dream, and not cultivating the least bit of merit and virtue. So how can they become Buddhas? They are 108,000 miles away from the Buddhas.

In other words, the merit and virtue we have cultivated is not as great as the offenses we have committed. You could say, "What we gain is not as much as what we lose," so how can we accomplish anything?

萬物皆在説法

明白了，就放下；
不明白，就執著。

各位！你們現在聽到《華嚴經》上説：佛示現百
千億種音聲，爲眾生演説妙法。我們應該覺悟世
界所有一切的聲音，皆在説法。所謂：

> 溪聲盡是廣長舌，
> 山色無非清淨身。

溪的聲音好像佛的廣長舌相，演説妙法；青山的
顏色，都是清淨法身，令視者生歡喜心。若能明
瞭這個道理，世上一切的一切，都在説法。

善人給你説善法，惡人給你説惡法，馬給你説做
馬的法，牛給你説做牛的法，令你明白爲什麼做
馬和做牛的因緣。原來馬、牛在前生的時候，不
孝順父母，不恭敬師長，或者不願聽父母或師長

All the Myriad Things Are Speaking the Dharma

If you understand, you can put it down. If you don't understand, you will be attached.

You all have heard that in the *Avatamsaka Sutra* it says, "The Buddhas manifest hundreds of thousands of millions of sounds to proclaim the wonderful Dharma for living beings." We should awaken to the fact that all the sounds in the world are speaking the Dharma. It is said,

> *The sounds of the brooks are all simply*
> *the vast, long tongue.*
> *The hues of the mountains are none other*
> *than the pure body.*

The sounds of the streams and creeks are just like the vast, long tongue of the Buddha, proclaiming the wonderful Dharma. The hues of the green mountains are all the pure Dharma-body, delighting those who see them. If you understand this principle, then absolutely everything in the world is speaking the Dharma.

Good people speak good Dharma for you, and bad people speak bad Dharma for you. Horses speak the Dharma of being a horse, and cows speak the Dharma of being a cow, enabling you to understand how they got to be horses and cows. As a matter of fact,

的訓誨，把身轉過去，脊背向著父母或師長，所以，今生做了畜生，也大同小異。

總而言之，持五戒、行十善，便生人天之界，有了貪瞋癡之心，便墮三惡道。

貓捕鼠、虎捉兔，弱肉強食，皆在說法。各有各的因果，各有各的立場，各說各的妙法。教授說教授的法，學生說學生的法。比丘說比丘的法，比丘尼說比丘尼的法。有情在說法，無情也在說法。若能認識，青山白雲，黃花翠竹，都在說法，萬事萬物皆在說法。

土匪去搶人家的錢財，因為在往昔，被他人所搶過，所以現在來討債；若是從前沒有被人搶過，如今去搶人家的財物，將來他要被人所搶，這是還債，這是因果循環報應真實的哲理。

所以人做事情要正大光明、大公無私，不可處處想佔便宜，不肯吃虧，所謂「吃虧就是佔便宜」，切記！切記！不應該佔方便，硬要去佔方便，

in their previous lives, horses and cows were probably people who were unfilial to their parents and disrespectful to their teachers. Perhaps they refused to listen to the admonishments of their parents and teachers, so they turned their backs to them. Now that they have become animals in this life, they are pretty much the same.

In general, if you observe the five precepts and practice the ten good deeds, you can be born in the human realm or the heavens. If you have greed, anger and stupidity in your mind, you will fall into the three evil paths.

Cats catch mice, tigers prey on rabbits, and the weak are eaten by the strong—these are all speaking the Dharma. Each has its own cause and effect, its own standing, and its own wonderful Dharma. Professors speak the Dharma of professors, and students speak the Dharma of students. Bhikshus speak the Dharma of Bhikshus, and Bhikshunis speak the Dharma of Bhikshunis. Sentient beings are speaking the Dharma, and insentient things are also speaking the Dharma. If you can recognize this, then the green mountains, the white clouds, the yellow flowers, and the green bamboo are all speaking the Dharma. All the myriad things and creatures are speaking the Dharma.

Robbers loot the wealth and property of other people because those people robbed them in previous lives, and they are now collecting the debt. If they weren't robbed in the past, and they rob the wealth and property of others now, they will be robbed in the future in order to pay their debt. That's the principle of retribution in the cycle of cause and effect.

Therefore, people should act in an upright way, be altruistic and

這是虧本。本來應該佔方便，而不去佔方便，這就是存款。

所以人要各正其位，各盡其職，不貪意外之財，不飲過量之酒，這也是説法。

　　　青青翠竹總是法身，
　　　鬱鬱黃花無非般若。

所以我們對於一切，應當如是觀。明白了，就放下；不明白，就執著。

unselfish. Don't try to take advantages. If you gain advantages by forcing it, you are actually taking a loss. It is said, "To take a loss is to gain an advantage." Keep that in mind, and don't forget it! If you're not supposed to gain an advantage, but you insist on getting it, you will just lose capital. If you're supposed to gain an advantage, and you don't try to get it, then you are putting a deposit in the bank.

Thus, each person should stand in his proper place and do his best to fulfill his obligations. You should not be greedy for unexpected wealth, nor should you drink too much alcohol. This is also speaking the Dharma.

> *The emerald-green bamboo is just the Dharma-body.*
> *The thriving yellow flowers are nothing but Prajna.*

That's how we should contemplate them. If you understand, you can put it down. If you don't understand, you will be attached.

莫待老來方學道

爲什麼到了現在，還要等待，
不去修行？

我們在這世界上，應該趕快修行，不要等待。年
輕時不修行，等到白頭時再修行，那就來不及了
，所謂：

> 莫待老來方學道，
> 孤墳盡是少年人。

年輕人也會很快就死去，不管老少，只要時候到
了，無常鬼就捉你去見閻羅王，這是一點也不客
氣的，所謂：

> 陽間無老少，
> 陰間常相逢。

各位注意！光陰很寶貴，一寸時光，就是一寸命
光，不要隨隨便便把光陰空過，等三災來臨的時
候，我們能否受得了？趁現在年輕時，要發奮修

Don't Wait Until You're Old to Cultivate the Way

Why, even now, do we still want to put off cultivating?

When we are in this world, we should hurry and cultivate. Don't wait around. If you don't cultivate when young, and you wait until your hair turns gray to cultivate, it will be too late. The saying goes,

> *Don't wait until you're old to cultivate the Way.*
> *The lonely graves are full of young people.*

Young people will also die soon. Regardless of whether you are young or old, when the time comes, the ghosts of impermanence will drag you off to see King Yama. They won't show you any courtesy at all. It is said,

> *Age makes no difference in the realm of the living.*
> *For people constantly meet in the realm of the dead.*

Each of you should pay attention! Time is precious. An inch of time is an inch of life, so don't casually let the time pass in vain. When the three disasters are imminent, will we be able to survive? While we are still young, we must cultivate zealously. Don't wait until tomorrow to cultivate. The best way is to immediately start cultivating today.

行，不要等到明天才修行。今天及時修行，方為
上策。

有人想：「今天先不修行，等明天才修行。」明
天又等明天，等來等去，頭髮白了，眼睛花了，
耳朵聾了，牙也掉了，到了那個時候想修行，身
體不聽招呼，四肢不靈活，那時就苦不堪言。

各位要知道，我們活在世界上，好像沒有水的魚
，沒有多久的時間，便嗚呼哀哉！所謂：

> 是日已過，命亦隨減；
> 如少水魚，斯有何樂。
> 大眾！
> 當勤精進，如救頭然；
> 但念無常，慎勿放逸。

我們從無量劫以來，一直到現在，還不知修行，
生了又死，死了又生，這是很值得我們痛心。為
什麼到了現在，還要等待，不去修行？各位想一
想，時間不會等待，轉瞬之間，一生就結束了。

Someone is thinking, "I won't cultivate today. I'll put it off till tomorrow." Tomorrow, you'll put it off to the next day. You keep putting it off until your hair turns white, your eyes become blurry, your ears go deaf, and your teeth fall out. At that point, you want to cultivate, but your body won't obey, and your four limbs are no longer agile. It will be unspeakably bitter then.

You all should know that living in this world, we are like fish in a pond that is evaporating. We don't have much time left! As it is said,

> *This day is already done.*
> *Our lives are that much less.*
> *We're like fish in a shrinking pond.*
> *What joy is there in this?*
> *Great Assembly!*
> *We should be diligent and vigorous,*
> *As if our own heads were at stake.*
> *Only be mindful of impermanence.*
> *And be careful not to be lax.*

From beginningless eons in the past until now, we have not known to cultivate. We undergo birth and death, and after death, birth again. We should really be pained at heart about this. Why, even now, do we still want to put off cultivating? Each of us should think about it—time doesn't wait. In the twinkling of an eye, this life will be over.

愛欲是修道的絆腳石

我們還有這口氣在，就要對人好，
可是不應有情愛的思想摻在內。

生死愛情的海，就是障道的根本。修道人，無論
對人或對物，生出愛欲之心，都會障礙修道的發
展。詳言之：愛欲就是生死，生死就是愛欲，愛
欲就是生死之根。若是不破愛欲無明，終不能離
開生死大愛海。如何能離開生死？簡單得很，就
是「斷欲去愛」，別無他法。

修道人，不要有情愛的思想，更不能有情愛的行
為。對任何人，不要生出一種情愛心；有了情愛
，苦根不斷；有了情愛，生死不能了。

有人說：「人是有感情的動物，食色性也。」就
因為這樣，所以才要修道！在《四十二章經》上
說：

134

Love and Desire: The Stumbling Blocks in Cultivation

As long as we still have a breath left, we should be good to people, but there shouldn't be any thoughts of emotional love involved.

The sea of the emotional love of birth and death is the fundamental obstacle to the Way. If cultivators feel love and desire, whether for people or objects, it will hinder them from making progress in cultivation. To discuss it in detail, love and desire are just birth and death, and birth and death are just love. Love and desire are the root of birth and death. If you don't break through the ignorance of love, you can never escape the great sea of love which is birth and death. How can you escape birth and death? It's simple—just cut off desire and get rid of love. There is no other way.

Cultivators shouldn't have thoughts of emotional love, even less should they engage in acts of emotional love. Don't give rise to thoughts of emotional love for anyone, no matter who it is. Once you have emotional love, you cannot cut off the root of suffering. Once you have emotional love, you cannot put an end to birth and death.

Someone says, "Humans are creatures of emotion. The desires for food and sensuality are part of their nature." Precisely for that reason, we must cultivate the Way! The *Sutra in Forty-two Sections* says,

> 想其老者如母。長者如姊。少者如妹。
> 稚者如子。生度脫心。息滅惡念。

我們修道人，就須存這種的觀想。如果無情無愛，見到人是不是就把嘴堵起來，不理睬人呢？這樣也不對。我們不執著情愛，不生情愛之心，但還不能討厭人，也不能說我不愛人，我就憎恨人，這樣也不對。那麼，要怎樣才對？就是不愛，也不憎。不愛不憎為中道。

修道，修什麼道？就是修這個中道，對誰都是平等相待，慈悲為懷，但要謹慎行事，不可落在情愛樊籠裏。

各位注意！不要被情愛所迷惑。有人寫封信給你，你的心就好像小兔子在懷中，亂蹦亂跳，以為有人愛你，這是好事，其實這是想把你拖到地獄去！

各位善知識！要在這個地方用功夫，要真真實實地瞭解：「愛欲，是一件很麻煩的事。」從無始

Think of those women who are elderly as your mothers,
those who are senior to you as your elder sisters, those
who are junior to you as your younger sisters, and those
who are young as your children. Resolve to save them, and
quell unwholesome thoughts.

Cultivators should contemplate in that way. Does having no emotion and love mean we should keep our mouth shut and ignore people when we see them? No, that's also wrong. We shouldn't cling to emotional love, or have thoughts of love, but we shouldn't loathe people, either. You can't say, "I don't love people, so I'll hate people." That's wrong, too. Well, what's the right way to act? Neither love nor hate. Not loving and not hating is the Middle Way.

What is the Way that we are cultivating? We cultivate the Middle Way, by treating everyone equally, showing kindness and compassion to all. But we must be careful not to get trapped in the cage of emotional love.

All of you should pay attention! Don't let love confuse you. If someone writes you a letter, your heart thumps like a bunny hopping wildly in your chest—you think it's wonderful that someone loves you. In reality, that person is just trying to drag you into the hells!

All Good and Wise Advisors! You must apply your efforts here, and truly understand that love is a very troublesome affair. From beginningless eons until now, we have failed to end birth and death. Why? It's because we have been harmed by emotional love. Only

137

劫以來，生死不了，為什麼？就因為被「情愛」二字所害。若能「斷欲去愛」，才能超出三界，了生脫死。

凡是你所願意的，就是愛；你所討厭的，就是憎恨。我歡喜這個，就生出愛心；我厭惡那個，就生出憎恨心，這都是感情用事。修行人不應該用感情來處理一切事。可是也不能像關帝公似的，坐在那裏蹦著臉，給他叩頭，他也不理睬。對人要和藹，要有禮貌，不可貢高我慢，目空一切。

總之，對人要以慈悲為懷，方便為門，處處為人著想，令人生歡喜心，我們還有這口氣在，就要對人好，可是不應有情愛的思想摻在內。各位！切記切記！這是很重要的法門。

by cutting off desire and getting rid of love can we transcend the Triple Realm and be liberated from birth and death.

Whatever you are fond of, you love, and whatever you dislike, you hate. If I like this, then I have a thought of love. If I am annoyed by that, then I have a thought of hate. This is to deal with things on an emotional level. Cultivators should not handle matters emotionally. But nor should they be like Lord Guan Yü, sitting there with a wooden expression. Even if you bow to him, he'll ignore you. We should be amiable and courteous to people. We cannot be arrogant and look down on everyone.

In general, we should treat people with a spirit of kindness and compassion, and use expedient methods. We should always be considerate of others and make people happy. As long as we still have a breath left, we should be good to people, but there shouldn't be any thoughts of emotional love involved. Each one of you should be sure to remember this! This is a very important Dharma-door.

爲世界和平而努力

宇宙若充滿祥瑞之正氣，
地球就不會爆炸了。

現在的世界，是由許多的國家組織而成；一個國家，是由許多的家組織而成；一個家，又是由許多人組織而成。所以，每個人與世界所有的人，都有連帶關係。

世上的人心，若是清淨，沒有污染的思想，這世界一定和平無戰爭；反之，人人的心都染污，這世界也跟著壞了。這個道理，人人都曉得，可是不實行，明知故犯，實在可憐！

所謂好，要從心做起；
所謂壞，也從心做起。

現在的世界，已經到了朝不保夕的時候了。爲什麼？因爲地球快要爆炸，已經到萬分危險的程度。地球爲什麼要爆炸？因爲被「貪瞋癡」三毒的

Working Hard For World Peace

If the universe is filled with auspicious proper energy, then the earth will not blow up.

The modern world is made up of many countries. Each country is made up of many families. Each family is made up of many people. Therefore, each person is very closely related to all the other people in the world.

If the minds of the people in the world are pure and free of defiled thoughts, this world will certainly be peaceful and free of war. On the other hand, if every person's mind is defiled, the world will consequently go bad. Everyone knows this principle, but no one applies it. We all know it clearly and yet go against it. That's truly pitiful!

That which is called "good" begins with the mind,
That which is called "bad" also begins with the mind.

The modern world has already reached the point of impending death, when one cannot be sure in the morning whether there will be an evening! Why is this? It's because the planet is on the verge of blowing up; the danger has reached an extreme. Why is the earth about to blow up? Because it has been oppressed by the violent

戾氣所壓迫的緣故。地球如果毀滅，我們人類當
然也不存在。

但是世人還不研究這個問題，終日醉生夢死在混
光陰，猶不知危機重重。有人只顧目前的問題，
不想將來的處境，他們擔憂人類一天比一天多起
來，沒有飯吃，沒有衣穿，沒有屋住，沒有能源
，認為這是嚴重的問題，其實這些問題是小問題
，到時候，自然會解決。

我們的「生死」，才是大問題。在這一分鐘有，
在那一分鐘就沒有了，轉眼之間，生離死別之苦
便降臨。可是人人對這嚴重的問題，反而冷淡，
好像在作夢似的。「生從何處而來？死往何處而
去？」這個問題一概不知。那麼，知道了又怎麼
辦呢？唯一解救的辦法，就是「改惡向善」，改
造自己，不要有自私自利，要有慈悲心，一切為
眾生，學習菩薩的精神。

每個人的行為，乃是由心念來支配，令他到十法
界去。一念善，可以生天上；一念惡，可以墮地
獄，所謂：

forces of the three poisons: greed, anger, and stupidity. If the earth is destroyed, the human race will certainly not survive.

But the people of the world still refuse to face this situation. They still pass their time in drunkenness and die in a dream, totally oblivious to the crisis. Some are only concerned about what lies before them and have no regard for the future. They worry that the human population is increasing daily, and that there are people with no food to eat, no clothes to wear, no houses to live in, and no energy supply; they think that those are the most serious problems. Actually, those are relatively minor problems which will naturally resolve themselves in time.

Our birth and death is really the big problem. One minute we're here, but the next minute we're gone. In the twinkling of an eye, the suffering of separation while alive or when nearing death comes upon us. But people all treat this serious problem with indifference, as if it were a dream. Where did we come from when we were born? Where will we go when we die? We have no idea. Even if we understood the situation, what could we do? There's only one way to save ourselves, which is to correct our faults and go towards the good, to reform ourselves. We shouldn't be so selfish and greedy for personal profit. Be kind and compassionate and do everything for the sake of other living beings. We should imitate the spirit of the Bodhisattvas.

Each person's behavior is controlled by his thoughts, which cause him to enter the Ten Dharma Realms. With one good thought, one can be born in the heavens. With one evil thought, one can fall into the hells. It's said,

> 一念覺就是佛，
> 一念迷即眾生。

簡單說，一念利益眾生，就是菩薩；一念利益自己，就是眾生；一念能迴光返照，反求諸己，就是阿羅漢和辟支佛。選擇在你自己，背覺合塵是凡夫，背塵合覺是聖人，如反掌之易。

世界好或壞，乃由一念心而起。這是必然的道理。「人人心善，世界永住；人人心惡，世界毀滅。」佛教是勸人向善，瞭解因果，多做善功德，也就是不爭、不貪、不求、不自私、不自利、不打妄語，世界自然轉危爲安，所謂「一切唯心造」。心能造世界，心能毀世界，心能造天堂，心能造地獄。

家由人而成，人由妄想而成。要是能將惡的妄想改爲善的妄想，就是好人；要是將善的妄想改爲惡的妄想，就是壞人；這是好人與壞人的關鍵。

我們修行人要「勤修戒定慧，息滅貪瞋癡」，這

With one enlightened thought, you are a Buddha.
With one confused thought, you are a living being.

To put it simply, with one thought to benefit living beings, you are a Bodhisattva. With one thought to benefit yourself, you are a living being. With one thought of turning the light inwards to reflect on yourself, you are an Arhat or a Pratyekabuddha. The choice is yours. If you turn your back on enlightenment and unite with defilement, you are a common person. If you turn your back on defilement and unite with enlightenment, you are a Sage. It's as easy as turning your hand over.

Whether the world is good or bad also depends on a single thought. If every person's mind is good, the world will abide eternally. If every person's mind is bad, the world will be destroyed. This is the law of nature. Buddhism exhorts people to go toward the good, to understand cause and effect, to create abundant wholesome merit and virtue. That is, if people refrain from contention, greed, seeking, selfishness, self benefit, and lying, the danger in the world will naturally become peace. It's said, "Everything is made from the mind alone." The mind can create the world, and it can destroy the world. The mind can create the heavens, and it can create the hells.

Families are made up of people, and people are made up of idle thoughts. If you change evil idle thoughts into good idle thoughts, you become a good person. If you change good idle thoughts into evil idle thoughts, you become a bad person. That's the pivotal point between being a good person and a bad person.

Cultivators should diligently cultivate precepts, samadhi and

是基本條件。學佛法的人，首先要「諸惡莫作，
眾善奉行」，這也是基本條件。如果人人能如此
去實行，世界就會轉好，瑞氣增多，戾氣減少。
宇宙若充滿祥瑞之正氣，地球就不會爆炸了。

怎樣令世界安穩？唯一辦法，來正法道場學佛法
，悔過自新。人人改惡向善，世界就沒有三災八
難，人人和睦相處，無爭無貪，成為大同世界。

希望沒有宗教信仰的人士，為家為國為世界，放
下貪心，多為社會做點有福利的事業，要知道「
財是身外之物」，生帶不來，死帶不去。

惡人借著善人的光，這世界才沒有三毒的戾氣，
才不至毀滅。這個道理雖然很淺，但用功很深，
才能有效果。各位！要從「心」著手，改造世界
，化干戈為玉帛，令世界平安。

每個人的領袖，就是「心」。心若壞了，身體就
疾病叢生，或遭意外災難。我們要反省，要檢討

wisdom, and put greed, anger, and stupidity to rest. Those are basic requirements. People who study the Buddhadharma should first of all abstain from all evil, and offer up all good conduct. That is a basic requirement. If everyone can really practice in that way, the world will become good, the auspicious energy will increase, and the violent energy will decrease. If the universe is filled with auspicious proper energy, then the earth will not blow up.

How can we make the world peaceful and stable? There is only one way: to come to a Way-place of the Proper Dharma to study the Buddhadharma, reform your faults, and renew yourself. If everyone mends his ways and becomes good, the world will be free from the three calamities and the eight difficulties, and all people will live together harmoniously, without greed or contention, in a world of Great Unity.

I hope the people who have no religious faith will, for the sake of the family, the country, and the world, renounce greed and do some work for the welfare of society. You should realize that money is an external thing which you did not bring with you at birth, nor can you take with you when you die.

If the light of the good people can counteract the darkness of bad people, this world will be free of the violent forces of the three poisons and will not be on the verge of extinction. Although this principle is very simple, it requires a profound effort to apply it successfully. All of you! You must begin with the mind and reform the world, changing hostility into harmony and bringing peace to the world.

，如有罪過，趕緊懺悔！所謂：

> 彌天大罪，
> 一懺便消。

可是要有誠心來懺悔，才能消災，不可當作兒戲，白天做惡事，晚間懺悔，認爲可以消災。如果有這思想，罪不但不能消，反而更加一級，爲什麼？因爲知法犯法，不可饒恕。

The master of each person is his mind. If the mind is corrupt, the body will be plagued with sickness and prone to accidents and disasters. We must reflect within and examine ourselves. If we have faults we should hurry and repent! It is said,

> *Offenses that fill up the skies are dissolved by*
> *a single thought of repentance.*

But you must sincerely repent if you want to quell disasters. You can't treat it as a joke, doing evil during the day and repenting at night, thinking you can quell disasters. With that kind of attitude, instead of getting rid of your offenses, you only increase their severity. Why? It's because you deliberately break the law, and therefore, you cannot be forgiven.

剋期取證打禪七

要腳踏實地用功參禪，
得到真本領那才算！

今天是禪七的開始，希望大家努力來參禪，不可
錯過開悟的大好時光。

打禪七就是剋期取證。不可坐在禪凳上打妄想，
那就是辜負自己參加打禪七的初衷。打什麼妄想
呢？妄想有種種不同，總而言之，都是異想天開
、不著邊際。有的人打這種妄想：「我參加這次
禪七，希望能開悟，得到大智慧，開悟之後，我
將向世界宣布這個消息，令全世界的人都知道我
是開悟的人，對我恭而敬之。」

各位想一想，有這種思想的人，他是否能開悟？
我敢下斷語，絕對不會的！為什麼？因為這個人
剛坐在禪凳上，妄想紛飛，不是為求名，就是為
求利。在名利上打轉轉，焉能開悟呢？

150

Chan Sessions Are for Seeking Enlightenment in a Limited Time

You must plant your feet on solid ground, and diligently work at meditation. Only when you attain true skill will it count!

The Chan session starts today, and I hope everyone will work diligently and not pass up this marvelous opportunity to become enlightened.

A Chan session is held for the purpose of seeking to become enlightened in a fixed period of time. So don't sit on the meditation bench and indulge in idle thinking; that would not do justice to your purpose in attending the Chan session. What kinds of idle thoughts might you have? Delusive thoughts come in all varieties, but in general they are no more than flights of fancy and wishful thinking. Some people have the idle thought: "I hope I can get enlightened and attain great wisdom in this session. After I'm enlightened, I'll publicize it to the world, and everyone will know I am an enlightened person and treat me with great respect."

All of you should consider this: can a person who thinks like that get enlightened? I emphatically declare that it's impossible. Why? As soon as that person sits on the meditation bench, his idle thoughts come in droves, and if he's not idly thinking about seeking fame, he's idly thinking about how to make a profit. How can a person who is spun around by fame and profit become enlightened?

有的人打這種妄想：「我在這次禪七中，一定要開悟，我要做這次禪七開悟第一人，人家不開悟，唯獨我一個人開悟，這是多麼光榮的一件事！」甚至根本沒有摸著開悟的邊緣，卻冒充開悟，到處宣傳自己開悟了，來欺騙大家，令大家對他另眼相看，來個魚目混珠的騙局，這種思想多麼幼稚，令人嗤笑！希望大家不要有這種妄想，要腳踏實地用功參禪，得到真本領那才算！

有的人打這種妄想：「我要開悟，開悟就有人來供養我，我可以建個大廟，作為一方法主，信徒源源而來，親近、供養我，我成為大法師，名揚天下，婦孺皆知我是大名鼎鼎的法師。」可是大家要知道，不學無術，受人供養，是心不安理不得的。

坐禪的姿勢要正確，對身心皆有益處，否則失掉坐禪的意義。坐禪時，先將身心放鬆，不可緊張，最好結雙跏趺坐，這是基本的坐法。

何謂雙跏趺坐？就是先把左腿放在右腿的上邊，然後將右腿搬到左腿上邊，這又叫「金剛座」，是堅固不動的意思。過去諸佛皆以金剛座而成佛

Some people have this idle thought: "In this Chan session, I definitely have to get enlightened. I have to be the first person to get enlightened in this session. I'll be the one and only enlightened person, and no one else will get enlightened. How glorious that would be!" Without even getting close to being enlightened, he feigns it and announces everywhere that he is enlightened. He cheats people because he wants them to show him special favor. His plan is to "pass off fish-eyes as pearls." But his ideas are so childish that people will only despise and laugh at him. Hopefully no one will entertain such ideas. Rather, we should plant our feet firmly on the ground and apply our efforts in investigating Chan, so that we can attain real skill that counts!

Other people have this kind of idle thought: "I want to get enlightened, so people will make offerings to me. Then I can build a big temple, be the Dharma host of the area, and have lots of followers who come and make offerings. I'll be a great Dharma Master known throughout the world, and everyone will treat me as a high-class Dharma Master." However, you must know that if you really aren't as proficient and knowledgeable as you make out to be, and you receive people's offerings, your conscience will not rest easy.

When sitting in Chan, make sure your posture is correct. A correct posture benefits both body and mind. Without it, sitting in Chan loses its meaning. When you sit in meditation, first relax the body and mind. Don't tense up. It would be ideal to sit in full lotus, which is the basic posture.

To sit in full lotus, first put the left foot over the right thigh, and then move the right foot over the left leg. This is also called the vajra position, which means it is firm and unmoving. All the

。這種坐法，可以降伏天魔，可以制止外道，他們見到這種坐法，知難而退，不敢前來找麻煩。

結雙跏趺坐之後，眼睛觀鼻端，不可東張西望。所謂：

> 眼觀鼻，鼻觀口，口觀心。

這樣才能攝持身心，將心猿意馬拴住，不令它們向外奔馳。所謂：

> 專一則靈，
> 分歧則弊。

要端然正坐，就是腰要直，頭要正，不可前俯，不可後仰；不要向左歪，不要向右斜；好像大鐘一樣，四平八穩，不動不搖。不可像鐘擺那樣，東搖西晃。雙跏趺坐才合乎坐禪的姿勢。

初學禪的人，覺得不習慣，腿也痛，腰也痠，不要緊，咬緊牙關，忍耐一時，久了自然沒有這種現象，所謂「久坐有禪」，自然得到禪味。

什麼是禪味？就是得到禪定的快樂，得到輕安的滋味。這種滋味奧妙無窮，不可以心思，不可以

Buddhas of the past attained Buddhahood by sitting in the vajra position. In this sitting posture, one can subdue the demons from the heavens and counter those of other religions. When they see you in this position, they surrender and retreat, afraid to disturb you.

Once you are sitting in lotus posture, your eyes should contemplate your nose, and not look left and right.

> *The eyes contemplates the nose;*
> *The nose contemplates the mouth;*
> *The mouth contemplates the heart.*

This way, you can gather in the body and mind. The mind is like a monkey or a wild horse, and you must tie it up so it won't run away. It is said,

> *When one is concentrated, there is*
> * an efficacious result.*
> *When one is scattered, there is nothing.*

You should sit properly, with the back straight and the head up. Don't lean forwards, backwards, or to the left or right. Sit firm and steady like a large bell, not swaying or moving. Don't be like the bell clapper which swings back and forth. Full lotus is the proper posture for sitting in Chan.

Beginning Chan meditators who are not used to it may experience pain in their legs and soreness in the back. Don't worry. Just grit your teeth and be patient for a while, and these sensations will naturally subside. It is said, "With long sitting, there is Chan." You will attain the flavor of Chan.

What is the flavor of Chan? You attain the bliss of Chan samadhi, and taste the flavor of light ease. This flavor is inexhaustibly subtle

言議，得身歷其境的人，才能體會，才能領受，好像如人飲水，冷暖自知，只可意會，不可言傳。各位想要知道這種禪味是甜是苦？就要努力參禪，到了相當境界時，自然曉得其中之味！所以要參！參到水落石出時，就得到禪味。

「禪」不是說的，而是參的，所以禪宗是不立文字，教外別傳，直指人心，見性成佛的法門。

參禪的人，參到火候的時候，絕對不發脾氣，不與人爭論，到了無諍三昧的境界。也不求名，也不求利，看富貴成為花間的露水，看功名成為瓦上的霜片，頃刻就消逝無蹤。真正修行人遠離名利，不為名利動搖其心。

若想測驗人是否有修行？就看他所行所為是不是在名利上動腦筋？如果求名得不到就發脾氣，求利得不到也發脾氣，那個無明火，老虎神，比誰都厲害，這個人，不問可知，一定是名利中人。

清朝乾隆皇帝到鎮江金山禪寺欣賞長江的風光，他問法磬禪師：「長江一日有多少船往來？」禪師說：「只有兩條船往來。」乾隆不解地問：「

and wonderful, inconceivable and indescribable. Only those who have experienced it will understand and know, just as a person who drinks the water will know its temperature. This can only be experienced by the mind, and cannot be communicated by mouth. If you want to know if the flavor of Chan is sweet or bitter, work hard at investigating Chan, and when you reach a certain stage, you will discover the flavor yourself! So, you must investigate! Investigate until "stones peep out from the receding water" (the truth is brought to light), and then you'll know the flavor of Chan.

Chan must be investigated, not discussed. That's why the Chan School is not based on language. Transmitted outside the teaching, this Dharma-door points directly to the mind, so that one sees the nature and attains Buddhahood.

When Chan cultivators have achieved a certain amount of skill in their investigation, they definitely will not lose their temper or argue with people, because they have reached the state of the samadhi of non-contention. Nor will they seek fame or gain, because they will regard wealth and honor as being like dew, and fame and position like frost, disappearing in an instant. Real cultivators keep their distance from fame and gain, and don't let their minds get influenced by them.

If you want to evaluate a person's cultivation, see if his every move is motivated by the desire for fame and profit. Is he someone who seeks fame, and gets mad when he cannot obtain it? Does he lose his temper if his pursuit of profit is frustrated? Does the fire of his ignorance and his tiger-like spirit make him the toughest one around? If so, then you know without asking that this person is after fame and profit.

When the Emperor Qianlung of the Qing Dynasty went to Gold

你怎知道只有兩條船呢？」禪師說：「一條船爲名，一條船爲利。」

由此可知，凡是乘船的人，不是爲名，就是爲利，但不知求名者死在名上，求利者死在利上，最後兩手空空去見閻羅王，所謂：

萬般帶不去，

只有業隨身。

修道人，若是沒有脾氣，能忍辱，能耐苦，始堪成法器，能爲佛教棟樑之材，將佛教發揚光大；凡是愛發脾氣的人，就是破壞佛教，成爲害群之馬。

佛教剛在西方清淨之土種下菩提種子，現在已經萌芽，生出幼苗，希望大家做個好園丁，勤灌漑，常施肥，令它欣欣向榮，令它蒸蒸日上，將來開菩提花，結菩提果。

住在萬佛聖城裏的四眾，對於講話要特別注意，不可信口亂講，不可任意講是講非。萬佛聖城是修道清淨的聖地，不可有旁門左道的言論，大家

Mountain Chan Monastery in Zhenjiang to view the scenery of the Yangtze River, he asked Chan Master Faqing, "How many boats come and go on the Yangtze in one day?" The Chan Master replied, "Only two boats." Qianlung was puzzled, and asked him, "How do you know there are only two boats?" The Chan Master said, "One boat is out for fame, and the other boat is out for profit."

From this, we know that anyone who takes a boat is either out for fame or for profit. What they don't know is that those who seek fame die for fame and those who seek profit die for profit. In the end, they go to see King Yama empty-handed. As it is said,

> *You can't bring anything with you.*
> *Only your karma will follow you.*

If a cultivator has no temper, and can endure insult and suffering, he can be a Dharma vessel and a pillar of Buddhism who can help Buddhism to expand and prosper. But if he likes to lose his temper all the time, he will only harm Buddhism and be the black sheep of Buddhism.

Buddhism has just planted the seeds of Bodhi in the pure soil of the West, and now they have already sprouted and put forth tender shoots. I hope everyone will be a good gardener and diligently water them and fertilize them often, so that they thrive joyously and grow more flourishing every day. Then eventually the Bodhi blossoms will open and bear the fruit of Bodhi.

The four-fold assembly of residents at the City of Ten Thousand Buddhas should be especially cautious in their speech. Don't talk recklessly, and don't gossip about the faults of others. The City of Ten Thousand Buddhas is a pure and holy place for cultivation, and will not tolerate heterodox teachings. Right in front of the ten

要知道，面對萬佛，怎可以亂講話？謹記！

病從口入，禍從口出。

這是至理名言，說話要三思而後說，免得錯因果。說出的話，不但要負法律的責任，也要負因果的報應。

佛教是提倡「無我」的宗教，不允許相面、批八字的存在，更不相信風水，這些技倆與佛法相違背，背道而馳，所以禁止流通。如果相信這種法，那就「有我」的存在，一切爲我所有，一切爲我打算，有我無人，不合乎佛法。

佛教是教人不爭、不貪、不求、不自私、不自利、不妄語的宗教。可是看風水是教人爭、教人貪、教人求、教人自私、教人自利，甚至妄言，在一百天之內能發大財，能做大官。貪心的人，便相信他的話。可是大財未發之前，先破小財，送紅包作謝禮，這種說法不如叫人去搶銀行，馬上發大財，不需要一百天以後再發財。

再者，他知道有好風水，可以發財，可以陞官，爲什麼自己不用，等你去用？豈有此理！希望聰

thousand Buddhas, how can people speak so carelessly? Take heed!

> *Sickness enters through the mouth;*
> *Calamity comes out of the mouth.*

This familiar adage holds a lot of principle. We should think thrice before speaking, to avoid making mistakes in cause and effect. Not only are we legally responsible for what we say, we must also undergo the retribution according to the law of cause and effect.

Buddhism is a religion which teaches selflessness, so it prohibits fortune-telling, whether by looking at facial features or hexagrams. Even less should we believe in geomancy. Since these skills go against the Buddhadharma and oppose the Way, their propagation is curtailed. If you have faith in these dharmas, you still have a notion of self. You will think of things as being "mine" and always be thinking on behalf of "myself." But considering only yourself and no one else does not accord with the Buddhadharma.

Buddhism is a religion which teaches people not to contend, not to be greedy, not to seek, not to be selfish, not to pursue personal benefit, and not to tell lies. Geomancers, on the other hand, tell people to contend, to seek, to be selfish, and to pursue personal benefit. They may even lie by telling people they will strike it rich or be promoted to a high rank in the next hundred days. Greedy people believe their words. But before they strike it rich, they first have to make a donation to the geomancer as a token of appreciation. The geomancers might as well tell people to rob a bank and get rich instantly, without having to wait a hundred days.

Moreover, if the geomancer really knows of some favorable geomantic features conducive to striking it rich or getting a big promotion, why wouldn't he use them himself? Why would he want

明人，千萬不要上迷信的當，被老千所騙。

「醫卜星相」在佛教中是五邪命之一，不受歡迎。「醫」是醫生，替人治病。「卜」是算卦，預知休咎。「星」是觀星，觀星宿知吉凶。「相」是相面，知命運順或逆。這是迷信，要知道「人定勝天」的道理。

出家修道人，生死大事都不怕，何況這些小事？更不足為奇。出家人是超出數外，所謂：

> 超出三界外，
> 不在五行中。

這種批八字、看風水，是俗不可耐的人才相信，要曉得人一生的命運，由業力所感。我們人不要被氣秉所拘，不要被物欲所蔽，要自己創造命運，把握命運，命運可以改造，多行功德事，自然遇難呈祥，逢凶化吉，所謂：

> 但行好事，
> 莫問前程。

我們現在打禪七，就是創造自己的新生命。不迷

to wait for you to use them? That makes no sense! I hope intelligent people will not let themselves be swindled by superstition or cheated by these old crooks.

Doctors, diviners, astrologists, and physiognomists belong to one of the five types of livelihoods which are improper (for left-home people). Doctors treat sicknesses, diviners forecast good and ill, astrologers tell fortunes by looking at the stars, and physiognomists look at facial features to predict whether one's life will be smooth or difficult. These are all superstitions. We should understand that "human determination can overcome fate."

Cultivators who have renounced the home-life are not afraid of the great matter of birth and death; how much the less are these small matters worth their interest. People who leave the home-life can transcend their fate.

> *They transcend the three realms and*
> *are no longer in the five elements.*

Only people who are strongly attached to the world believe in such things as horoscopes and geomancy. We should know that a person's destiny is the result of his karma. We shouldn't let our temperament restrict us, or let our physical desires obscure our purpose. Instead, we ought to create our own destiny and take control of our destiny. We can change our destiny. If you do many meritorious and virtuous deeds, hardships will transform into auspiciousness. There is a saying,

> *Just practice good deeds,*
> *And don't ask about the future.*

Now as we attend the Chan session, we are establishing a new life.

信，而正信；不要人云亦云，以訛傳訛，不要跟著人家後面跑，這是大錯而特錯。要有擇法眼，知道是非，明白善惡，黑白分析清清楚楚，就不會顛顛倒倒了。

參禪的人，對於自己的生死能做主宰，來去自由，不受任何限制，所謂：

性命由我不由天

就是閻羅老子也管不了，對你無可奈何！為什麼呢？因為你已經出離三界的緣故。

何謂來去自由？也就是生死自由，愛活就活，愛死就死，遂心所欲。可是要注意，這種死並不是自殺，也不是服毒。

我們的身體，好像房子，願意出外旅行，到什麼地方去，都是自由。願意化身千百億，盡虛空、遍法界去教化眾生，任運自如。不願意旅行，就在房子住，沒有人來干涉。要曉得盡虛空、遍法界，都在法身中，沒有跑到法身之外邊。

大家辛辛苦苦來參禪，晝夜不停來用功，就希望

Get rid of superstition, and believe in what's proper. Don't just repeat what you hear and go around spreading lies. Don't blindly follow behind others—that would be a great mistake. You must have the Dharma-selecting Eye so that you can tell right from wrong, understand what's good and what's evil, and distinguish clearly between black and white. Then you won't be turned upside-down in confusion.

Those who investigate Chan can be the masters of their own birth and death. They can come and go freely without any restriction. As it is said,

My destiny is determined by myself, not by heaven.

Even Old Man Yama has no control over you. He cannot touch you! Why not? Because you've already transcended the Three Realms.

What is meant by being free to come and go? It is the freedom to be born and die. If you want to live, you can live; if you want to die, you can die, as your heart desires. But take note—this kind of death doesn't mean committing suicide or taking poison.

Our body is like a house, and if we want to go out and travel, we are free to go wherever we want. If we wish, we can have a hundred million transformation bodies to teach living beings throughout empty space and the Dharma Realm. If we don't wish to travel, we can stay in the house and no one will disturb us. We should know that everything in empty space and in the Dharma Realm is included within the Dharma-body. Nothing can go outside the Dharma-body.

All of you have gone to a lot of trouble to come attend the Chan session, and to work non-stop day and night, because you hope to gain freedom and security over birth and death, to control your own

生死自由，能控制自己的生命，對生死有把握，能做得主，那才是得到生死自由的境界。

參禪的人，參到上不知有天，下不知有地，中不知有人，與虛空合而爲一，到了這種境界，便有開悟的曙光了。行行坐坐，坐坐行行，便是開智慧的鑰匙。

參「念佛是誰？」念佛是哪一個？哪一個在念佛？打坐是哪一個？哪一個在打坐？吃飯，是哪一個吃飯？睡覺，是哪一個睡覺？要來找這個人，找就是參，參到山窮水盡，一轉身便是開悟時，所謂：

> 山窮水盡疑無路，
> 柳暗花明又一村

故云：

> 百尺竿頭重進步，
> 十方世界現全身。

如果不參禪，不打坐，生從何處來？死往何處去？他說不知道。不知道，就糊糊塗塗生來，又糊塗塗塗死去，這樣一輩子，多麼可憐！

life, and to be your own master. That is truly the state of freedom over birth and death.

In investigating Chan, when you reach the state of not knowing that there is the sky above, the earth below, and people in between, and you become one with empty space, there is some hope for enlightenment. Walking and sitting, sitting and walking—these are the key for opening our wisdom.

Investigate "Who is mindful of the Buddha?" Which person is mindful of the Buddha? Who is sitting in meditation? Which person is sitting in meditation? Who is the one eating? Who is the one sleeping? We must search for that person. To search, we must investigate. When we investigate to the point that the mountains disappear and the waters vanish, all we have to do is turn around and we'll be enlightened. There is a saying,

> When the mountains disappear and the waters vanish,
>   you doubt there is a road ahead.
> Beyond the dark willows and the bright flowers
>   is another village.

It is also said,

> If you can climb to the top of a hundred-foot pole
>   and then take another step,
> The worlds in the ten directions
>   will appear in their entirety.

If you don't investigate Chan and sit in meditation, where do you come from when you are born? Where will you go when you die? You don't know. Not knowing, you are born in a muddle and you die in a muddle, and you spend your whole life the same way. How pitiful!

用功參禪的人，開了悟，認識父母未生之前的本來面目。豁然貫通，則眾物之表裏精粗無不到，而吾心之全體大用無不明。得到大造大化的境界，將來能成就佛果，無上正等正覺的地位。

老子曾經說過這兩句話：

> 天下皆知美之為美，斯惡已。
> 皆知善之為善，斯不善已。

世界的人，都知道做美好的事情是好的，可是到做的時候，就不美了。人人都說做善事是對的，可是境界來了，受不住考驗，被境界所誘惑，就不做善事，而去做惡事。

學佛法的人，明知「慈悲喜捨」四無量心，是行菩薩道的基本法，可是不去行。那麼，明白道理又有什麼用處？天天學「六度」法，等到境界來了，布施也不布施，持戒也不持戒，忍辱也不忍辱，精進也不精進，禪定也不禪定，智慧也不智慧，你說有什麼用？

（一）布施：是用財法布施於人，可是境界來了，就不布施了，相反叫人布施給自己，越多越好

If you work hard at investigating Chan, then when you get enlightened you will recognize your original face before your parents gave birth to you. You will suddenly fathom everything: you will know all the internal and external details and general and subtle aspects of all the myriad phenomena, and you will thoroughly comprehend the total functioning of the mind. Having attained the state of great creation and great transformation, you will eventually accomplish the Buddha fruition and attain the highest proper, equal, right enlightenment.

Laozi once said,

> *When all the world knows what is fine,*
> *then what is bad already exists.*
> *When they know what is good,*
> *then what is not good already exists.*

The people of the world all know that it is good to do fine, wholesome deeds, but when it comes time to do them, they are no longer fine. Everyone says it's right to do good deeds, but when states come, they can't pass the test. Confused by states, they do evil deeds instead of good ones.

Students of the Buddhadharma know the Four Boundless Minds—kindness, compassion, joy, and giving—are fundamental to the practice of the Bodhisattva path, yet they don't practice them. What use is it if you just understand the theory? Every day you study the Six Perfections, but when the situation comes, you don't practice giving, you don't hold the precepts, you aren't patient, you aren't vigorous, you don't cultivate Chan samadhi, and you don't use wisdom. Tell me, what use is that?

1. Giving: You are supposed to give wealth to others, but when you're in a situation to do so, you don't give. On the contrary, you

。我不布施於你，你要布施於我，要佔便宜，不想吃虧，這種人比比皆是。

（二）持戒：天下人皆知持戒爲持戒，可是境界來了，不但不能持戒，反而毀戒。守戒就是不動心；無論什麼境界來了，無動於衷，就是「泰山崩前心不驚，美色當前心不動」，有這種的定力，就能轉境界，不管善惡順逆的境界，皆處之泰然，不生分別心，自然風平浪靜。

（三）忍辱：忍受一切不如意的事，這就是考驗。經得起考驗，便能過關；經不起考驗，就過不了關。人人皆知忍辱能到彼岸，可是境界來了，就忍不住，無明火高三千丈，將多年來所積聚的功德，燒得一乾二淨。

（四）精進：打禪七就是精進。人人想精進，到了精進的時候，就不精進。躲懶偷安向後退，跑到一邊去泡茶，或者故意到廁所方便，或者故意到廚房飲茶，這都是藉口混時間。在沒有打禪七之前，說得很好聽，我一定要好好打這個禪七。等到禪七開始，就不聽話了，把以前自己所立之誓言，都推翻了，爲什麼？明知故犯。知道參禪

demand that others give to you, the more the better. "I won't give you anything, but you should give me something. I should gain the advantage, not take a loss." That's the attitude everyone has.

2. Holding Precepts: The whole world knows that holding precepts means holding precepts, but when states come, people break the precepts instead of holding them. Holding the precepts means not letting one's mind be moved. No matter what state you meet, your mind docs not move. Even when Mount Tai has a landslide, you are not startled. When a beautiful woman passes in front of you, you are not affected. With that kind of samadhi, you can turn states around. Whether the state is good or bad, pleasant or adverse, you remain calm and composed. When you don't give rise to discriminations, the wind calms down and the waves naturally subside.

3. Patience: You have to patiently endure the things which don't turn out the way you wish them to. This is a test. If you pass, then you have jumped over the hurdle. If you fail, then you haven't made it over the hurdle. Although we all know that patience can take us to the other shore, when we meet a difficult state, we cannot be patient. Then the fire of ignorance blazes up and burns away all the merit and virtue we accumulated over the years.

4. Vigor: Attending the Chan session is being vigorous. Everybody would like to be vigorous, but when the time comes, you aren't vigorous. Trying to be lazy and take a break, you slack off in your cultivation and run outside to make some tea. Or maybe you go to the restroom or to the kitchen to drink tea—these are all excuses to waste time. Before the session started, you say, "I'm going to work really hard in this Chan session." But after the session starts, you don't act that way. You overturn all your former resolves. You deliberately break them. You know investigating

是好，可是還要懶惰，你說有這種矛盾的心理怎麼辦？禪堂的規矩，不守規矩，打香板，打！打！打到開悟爲止。

（五）禪定：現在參禪，正是用功的好時光。爲什麼要打禪七？就是教你精神集中，心無妄想，令智慧現前，所謂「智慧解脫」，也就是剋期取證的法門。

（六）智慧：也能到彼岸，也能了生死。可是剛剛要開智慧，他就懈怠了，而錯過開悟的機會，所以參禪要分秒必爭，不知在哪一分鐘就開悟。有人打妄想，我不要智慧，我的愚癡很好啊！不明白一切事理，就算了嘛！這是掩耳盜鈴，自己騙自己，到了死的時候，才覺悟白來世間一趟，悔之晚矣！

佛教在這個國家（美國）正是開始的時候，需要有眞眞實實的修行人，要躬行實踐。要專一其心地修行，要改過自新地修行，要破除習氣地修行，爲旁人的榜樣，這樣佛教的前途就光明。如果一開始，就沒有眞正修行人作爲模範，沒有發大菩提心者，那麼，佛教在西方也不會興盛起來。

Chan is good, but you still want to be lazy. How should we deal with such a contradictory mind? Anyone who doesn't abide by the rules of the Chan Hall will be beaten with the stick—bam! bam! bam!—until they get enlightened.

5. Chan Samadhi: Now you are investigating Chan, and you should make full use of the time to apply effort. Why are you attending the Chan session? It is because you want to concentrate your mind until there are no more idle thoughts, so that your wisdom can manifest. This is known as the "liberation of wisdom," and in this Dharma-door you aim for achievement in a limited time.

6. Wisdom: Wisdom enables you to reach the other shore and end birth and death. But if a person gets lazy right at the point when his wisdom is about to come forth, he'll miss the chance to become enlightened. In the investigation of Chan, you must apply effort in every minute and every second, because you don't know which particular instant you might get enlightened. Someone is thinking, "I don't want to have wisdom; my stupidity is just fine. If I don't understand anything, so be it!" You are just trying to fool yourself. When it's time to die, you'll realize you've wasted your whole life, but by that time it's too late for regret.

Buddhism is just beginning in this country (United States), and needs to have true cultivators, people who really practice. We must cultivate by concentrating single-mindedly; we must cultivate by changing our faults and renewing ourselves; we must cultivate by smashing through our bad habits and being a good model for others. If we can do that, Buddhism is sure to have a bright future. But if at the start there aren't any true cultivators who can serve as good models, and no one makes a great resolve for Bodhi, Buddhism will not be able to prosper in the West. So the prosperity or failure of

所以佛教興衰的責任，要你們青年人負起這個重擔。

現在三步一拜果眞（恆實）和果廷（恆朝）這樣誠心地修行，給佛教作爲開路的先鋒。他們在路上三步一拜，不是爲自己求福報，而是爲世界求和平。兩年多以來，忍飢忍渴，忍寒忍熱，忍風忍雨，這樣地苦修，非一般人所能做到的。他們能忍人所不能忍的，能讓人所不能讓的，能吃人所不能吃的，能穿人所不能穿的，不管颶風下雨，照拜不誤，不管寒暑飢渴，不休息不懈怠，每天照常做早晚課，一時一刻也不躲懶偷安。他們這樣地發奮，就想將佛教推行到全世界去，令它發揚光大。這兩位行者，如此辛苦，不是圖名，不是貪利，而是以發展佛教爲已任。這種精神可嘉可勉！

你們應該向三步一拜二行者看齊，作爲借鏡。照照自己，反省一下，對佛教有什麼貢獻？我所行所作是爲自己還是爲佛教？如果爲自己，就應該生大慚愧心，立刻糾正這種不當的行爲；若是爲佛教，更要努力，再接再厲，推行佛教，維護佛教，要認眞發菩提心，無企圖行菩薩道，一切爲

Buddhism is a great burden which all of you young people must bear.

Guo Zhen (Heng Sure) and Guo Ting (Heng Chau), who are now sincerely cultivating on a "three steps, one bow" pilgrimage, are the trailblazing pioneers of Buddhism. They take three steps and bow down on the road, not seeking blessings for themselves, but peace for the world. For more than two years, they have endured hunger, thirst, cold, heat, wind and rain. This kind of bitter cultivation is not something most people can do. They endure what others cannot endure, yield what others cannot yield, eat what others cannot eat, and wear what others cannot wear. Even in the wind and rain, they never miss a bow. In spite of the heat, cold, hunger, and thirst, they never stop to rest. Every day they do the morning and evening ceremonies as usual, not allowing themselves to be lax at any moment. The reason they are so energetic is because they wish to spread Buddhism and make it flourish all over the world. These two cultivators are working so arduously, not out of greed for fame or profit, but because they feel personally responsible for propagating Buddhism. Their spirit is truly commendable, and should be encouraged.

All of you should strive to be like these "three steps, one bow" cultivators. When you see their example, you should ask yourself, "What have I contributed to Buddhism? Do I do everything for my own sake, or for the sake of Buddhism?" If everything I do is for my own sake, I ought to be greatly ashamed and immediately correct my improper behavior. If it is for Buddhism, I should work even harder, and make a determined effort to propagate and support Buddhism. I should earnestly make the resolve to seek Bodhi, and practice the Bodhisattva Way without any expectations or desires. In everything I do, I should make the peace and happiness of others

人得安樂作前提，不爲自己利益作打算，這才是菩薩的精神。

你們在禪堂裏，跑跑坐坐、坐坐跑跑，覺得很辛苦，若和三步一拜他們的辛苦來比較，那是自在多了。關於這一點，要深深地體會，不要當面錯過，交臂失之。這兩位行者，若是不發菩提心，不行菩薩道，根本就不能堅持拜到底。

你們在禪堂裏，不要打妄想，身在禪堂中，心到世界去觀光，這樣胡思亂想，會影響修道之心。切記！不要把光陰空過，要把握時機，迎接開悟來臨！這樣的準備，才能對得起自己；否則，一切空談。

一九七九年八月二十日開示於萬佛聖城

my top priority, and not scheme for my own benefit. That's the true spirit of a Bodhisattva.

You are walking and sitting, sitting and walking, and you think it's very grueling, but it's much more comfortable than the toil of bowing every three steps. You should deeply realize this, and not let this opportunity go by in vain. If those two cultivators hadn't made the Bodhi resolve to practice the Bodhisattva Way, they would find it impossible to persist and bow to the very end.

While in the Chan Hall, don't entertain any idle thoughts. If you do, then although your body is in the hall, your mind is out sightseeing in the world. Those reckless and confused thoughts will affect your resolve to cultivate. By all means, don't waste time. Use your time well and draw closer to enlightenment. If you prepare yourself in this way, you won't be sorry. But if you don't, it's all just empty words.

A talk given on August 20, 1979
in the City of Ten Thousand Buddhas

恰到好處是中道

緊了繃，慢了鬆，
不緊不慢才成功。

參禪的法門，要念茲在茲。時時刻刻都要迴光返照，也不要緊，也不要慢，所謂：

> 緊了繃，慢了鬆，
> 不緊不慢才成功。

不緊不慢就是中道，行住坐臥不離這個，離了這個，就是錯過。這個是什麼，就是中道了義。

參禪要不偏不倚，不要太過，也不要不及，太過或不及，那不是中道。不落空有二邊，才是中道。所謂「中道就是非空非有」，也就是真空妙有。無著於真空，無礙於妙有，真空妙有不可取，也不可捨，取也不得，捨也不可，這是真空妙有的境界。

178

Doing It Just Right
is the Middle Way

Too tight, and it'll break. Too slack, and it'll be loose. Neither tight nor slack, and it will turn out right.

In the Dharma-door of investigating Chan, you must fix your attention on what you are doing. At all times, you should return the light and reflect within. Don't be too tense, and don't be too slack. It's said,

> *Too tight, and it'll break. Too slack, and it'll be loose.*
> *Neither tight nor slack, and it will turn out right.*

Being neither tense nor slack is the Middle Way. Walking, standing, sitting and lying down, don't be apart from this. Once you leave this, you have missed it. What is this? It's the ultimate meaning of the Middle Way.

In investigating Chan, you must be impartial, not leaning to one side. Don't go too far, and don't fail to go far enough. If you go too far, or not far enough, it's not the Middle Way. If you don't fall into the two extremes of emptiness and existence, then that's the Middle Way. It's said, "The Middle Way is neither emptiness nor existence." It is True Emptiness and Wonderful Existence. Do not be attached to true emptiness, and do not be obstructed by wonderful existence, for true emptiness and wonderful existence cannot be grasped or renounced. You cannot take hold of them or let go of them. That's the state of true emptiness and wonderful existence.

用功的人，要有始有終，才能有所成就，所謂「貫徹始終」。不可一曝十寒，遇難即退，半途而廢，那是沒有出息的人，古人說：

> 修道不怕慢，只怕站。

平時用功參禪，照顧自己的話頭，用自己的金剛寶劍（智慧），斬斷一切的妄想；妄想斬斷，智慧現前；有了智慧光明，破了無明的黑暗；無明破除，就出離三界，不受生死，也就是闖過生命之輪（十二因緣）的關。

用功修道的人，要有忍耐心，無論怎樣辛苦，都要忍受，忍就能到彼岸，所以各位打禪七，不要怕辛苦，所謂「苦盡甘來」。「不在最底下，到不了最頂上。」要知道萬丈高樓乃是從平地建起，不是在虛空造成的。所以我們參禪的人，要從根本上入手，就是把妄想驅除。若能把妄想制止，這時候，

> 心清水現月，
> 意定天無雲。

When you are applying effort, you should finish what you start; only then will you accomplish anything. As it's said, "Carry it through from beginning to end." You shouldn't "put it in the sun for one day and freeze it for ten," retreat in the face of difficulty, or give up halfway—that's the behavior of people without backbone. The ancients said,

> In cultivation, don't be afraid to go slowly.
> Just be afraid of standing still.

In your daily investigation of Chan, be mindful of your own meditation topic, and slash through all your idle thoughts with your Vajra-jewelled sword of wisdom. When idle thinking is severed, wisdom will arise. With the light of wisdom, you can smash through the gloom of ignorance. Once ignorance is smashed, you can transcend the Three Realms, escape birth and death, and crash your way out of the wheel of life (i.e. the twelve links of conditioned co-production).

Those who apply effort in cultivating the Way must have patience. No matter how hard it is, you must patiently bear it. With patience you can reach the other shore. So in joining this Chan Session, you all should not be afraid of hardship. It's said, "When bitterness ends, sweetness comes." If you don't start at the very bottom, you can't reach the top. Remember that a ten thousand foot skyscraper is built from the ground up. It isn't built in mid-air. Therefore, Chan cultivators must start with the basics, which are to get rid of idle thinking. If you can stop your idle thoughts, then at that point,

> The moon appears in the waters of a pure heart;
> There are no clouds in the sky of a calm mind.

心平百難皆散，意定萬事皆平，所謂：

> 心止念絕眞富貴，
>
> 私欲斷盡眞福田。

參禪就是去妄存眞，也就是沙裏澄金，在沙子裏找金粒，那是很不容易的一件事。可是你想求金子，必須在沙子裏找，必須要有耐性，你想明白自己本有佛性嗎？明心見性嗎？就要有耐心去修行，去參學，去研究，久而久之，豁然貫通，驟然開悟，原來如此！

參禪上了路，不需要打閒岔，各位自己努力參「念佛是誰？」非把這個「誰」找到不可，什麼時候找到，方可停止。功夫到了爐火純青的時候，便有好消息。

結雙跏趺坐的姿勢，是將左腿放在右腿上，然後將右腿搬到左腿上，因爲左腿屬於陽，右腿屬於陰。打坐時，左腿是陽在上邊，右腿是陰在下邊，好像無極生太極，太極生兩儀（陰儀、陽儀），也是這樣的擺法。若是因爲方便起見，左腿在

When the heart is at peace, all problems go away: When the mind is still, the myriad things are in harmony. As it is said,

> *True wealth is stopping the mind and*
> *cutting off thought:*
> *True fields of blessings are devoid*
> *of all selfish desires.*

One investigates Chan just to get rid of the false and keep the true. It is also to pan for gold, to look for gold dust in the sand, which is a difficult task. But if you want to find gold, you have to look in the sand, and be patient. Do you want to understand your inherent Buddha-nature? Do you want to understand your mind and see your nature? Then you must patiently cultivate, study and investigate, and when enough time has passed, you will suddenly penetrate and enlighten to the fact that it is originally this way!

When your investigation of Chan is progressing well, there's no need to meddle in other people's business. Each of you should put forth effort to investigate "Who is mindful of the Buddha?" No matter what, you have to find out "who" it is. Only when you find the answer can you stop. When the intensity of your efforts has reached a peak, there will be good news.

To sit in full-lotus posture, put your left foot on your right thigh, and then put your right foot on your left thigh. The reason for this is that the left leg is *yang* and the right leg is *yin*. When you sit in meditation, the left leg which is *yang* is on top, and the right leg which is *yin* is below. This is like the Limitless giving rise to the Absolute, and the Absolute giving rise to the two primordial forms (the *yin* fish and the *yang* fish)—they are also set up in this way.

下，右腿在上也可以的。法無定法，隨著個人習慣而決定，不必執著一定要這種姿勢。教你左腿壓右腿，這只是個方法而已。並不是硬性規定，一定要這樣子。

總而言之，結跏趺坐，是教你容易入定。你能在走路時入定，那麼坐不坐都可以的。入定的境界，沒有任何的妄想，心中一念不生，一塵不染。若能行住坐臥一念不生，一塵不染，那就是在用功，並不一定是坐在那裏，才算是用功。

For the sake of convenience, putting the left leg below and the right leg on top is also okay. The Dharma is not fixed, and the decision is based on individual preference. You don't need to become attached and think that you have to use this posture. When I teach you to put your left leg on top of your right leg first, that's only one method. It's not a hard and fast rule that you have to do it that way.

In general, sitting in the full-lotus posture will make it easier for you to enter samadhi. If you can remain in samadhi even when you are moving, then it is not necessary to sit. Within samadhi, you have no idle thoughts. Your mind is totally free from thinking and you are not defiled by even a speck of dust. If you can constantly maintain this state when you are moving, still, sitting or reclining, then you are working vigorously. It is not the case that you are working hard only when sitting.

佛法最平等

在佛教裏，一分功，一分過，
絲毫不會差錯。

佛法是很微妙的，在佛法裏，感覺不到有什麼好
處，在佛法外，也不覺得有什麼壞處。可是在佛
教裏，一分功，一分過，絲毫不會差錯。佛教裏
，亦是最自由、最平等，沒有專制，毫不偏袒。

為什麼說最平等呢？因為一切眾生，無論餓鬼地
獄，凶神惡獸，惡人壞人，如果肯發心修行，回
頭是岸，都可成佛。不像外道說：「惡人壞人，
永遠都壞，無法可度；猛虎惡獸，性情殘暴，亦
不可救。」

中國明朝時代，有蓮池大師，他便收了一隻老虎
徒弟，護持左右。可是老虎是惡獸，人見人怕，
所以大師就教牠出入不要直行，虎亦遵命，出入
退行，人們也就不怕，知為善虎。老虎徒弟還會

The Buddhadharma is Completely Fair

In Buddhism, the retribution you receive for each share of merit and each share of offense you create will not be off by a hairsbreadth.

The Buddhadharma is very subtle and wonderful. When you are inside the Buddhadharma, you can't detect any advantage, and when you are outside the Buddhadharma, you don't feel any disadvantage. But in Buddhism, the retribution you receive for each share of merit and each share of offense you create will not be off by a hairsbreadth. In Buddhism, there is also the greatest freedom and the greatest equality. It is not despotic or biased in the least.

Why is it said to be equal? It's because if any living being, whether it's a hungry ghost, hell-being, evil spirit, ferocious beast, wicked person, or bad person, brings forth the resolve to cultivate, then "a turn of the head is the other shore," and that being can become a Buddha. Buddhists are unlike externalists who advocate that bad or wicked people are eternally bad and beyond redemption, and that ferocious tigers and evil beasts, being wild by nature, cannot be saved.

During the Ming dynasty, there was the Great Master Lianchi who accepted a tiger as his disciple. This tiger disciple accompanied him around and protected him. As tigers are known to be vicious beasts, everyone was terrified upon seeing it. Thereupon Great Master Lianchi told the tiger to walk backwards instead of forward. When

到各處爲蓮池大師化緣。人們見到善虎，還爭相
布施供養呢！所以虎亦能皈依三寶，護持佛法，
亦可成佛。

佛教最自由，因佛教裏，只是勸人行善，不要做
惡。做惡會自作自受，自取其報。但佛教不會強
迫人去行善，亦不會說，你不聽話，專造惡業，
我會造一所牢獄把你關進去。因爲一切唯心造，
天堂、地獄，皆是依人的思想和業力造成。故佛
法教人「諸惡莫作，眾善奉行」，並闡明絲毫不
爽的因果律，教人認識眞理而超出輪迴。

the tiger did this, the people felt assured that it was tame, and they were no longer afraid of it. The tiger went everywhere to raise funds for the Great Master. People all crowded in to make offerings when they saw this good tiger coming. So it is said that tigers can also take refuge with the Triple Jewel, protect the Buddhadharma and become Buddhas.

Buddhism gives people the greatest freedom, because in Buddhism, people are only exhorted to practice good deeds and abstain from evil deeds. If you do evil, you yourself must suffer the retribution. But Buddhism doesn't force people to do good, and would not say, "If you don't listen, and you keep making bad karma, I'll build a prison and lock you up in it." That's because everything is made from the mind alone. The heavens and the hells are created based on people's thoughts and the force of their karma. Thus the Buddhadharma teaches people to "Abstain from all evil and offer up all good conduct," and explains the law of cause and effect, which never misses by even a hairsbreadth. It teaches people to recognize the truth and transcend the cycle of birth and death.

大善大惡，超出數外

命運是可以改造的，
操之在自己手中。

從前有一個人，名叫袁了凡，他本名袁學海，是明朝的名儒，小時候就讀書，可是父親要他學醫，濟世救人，所以改學醫。後來遇到一長鬚老相士對他說：「你命帶官印，你應該讀書可做大官。某年某月某日可考中秀才，某年某日可作縣官，俸祿多少。某年某日陞官，俸祿多少。到五十四歲八月十四日半夜子時壽終正寢，終生無子。」於是乎袁學海就轉讀書，一切都如算者所言中，十分靈驗。既然命中是註定，所以他就等命運安排，受命運支配，不求上進，終日遊山玩水。

有一天，遊到南京棲霞山，聞有雲谷禪師，他就上山參訪。禪師給他一個蒲團，二人無言對坐三天。雲谷禪師很驚奇說：「你從何處來？能夠三天安坐不動不打妄想，是有道奇人也。」

Great Good and Great Evil Can Transcend Fate

**Fate can be changed, and the power
to do so is in our own hands.**

Once there was a man named Yuan Liaofan, who was originally named Yuan Xuehai and was a famous Confucian scholar in the Ming Dynasty. He pursued scholarly studies in his youth, but because his father wanted him to learn medicine in order to save the world's people, he changed his course of study to medicine. Later, he met an old, long-haired diviner of physiognomy who told him, "It is your fate to become an official. You should pursue scholarly learning, for then you can become a great official. On a certain day, month, and year, you can pass the examination and become a graduate of the first degree. On a certain day and month, you can become a district magistrate with a salary of so much. On a certain day of a certain year, you will be promoted and your salary will become so much. At midnight on August 14th of your fifty-fourth year, your life will come to an end. You will have no sons." Thereupon, Yuan Xuehai changed his course and pursued scholarly studies, and everything turned out as the diviner had predicted. It was completely accurate. Since he thought his destiny was fixed, he just waited for fate to take its course. He was ruled by fate, and did not seek to improve himself. Instead, he spent his days traveling and enjoying the scenery of mountains and rivers.

One day he traveled to Qixia Mountain in Nanjing, and hearing that

191

袁學海就說：「既然什麼事都是命中註定，所以我就不貪、不求、不妄想。」

雲谷禪師說：「我還以為你是非常人，原來只是凡夫俗子。」

袁學海不高興說：「為什麼說我是凡夫俗子？」

雲谷禪師曰：「如果不是凡夫，為什麼被命運所縛？」

袁學海就問：「命運可逃嗎？」

雲谷禪師回答：「你是讀書人，《易經》上不是說得清清楚楚『趨吉避凶』，如果命數不可逃，那怎麼可以趨吉避凶呢？」

袁學海大悟，所以改名為「了凡」，意思就是從今天起，已不是凡人了。從此以後，他廣行善事，多積功德。如此一來，以前相者所說的，都不靈驗，並且活到八十多歲，又有三個兒子。所以命運不是一定的，凶吉也不是一定的，古人說：

the Chan Master Yunku was there, he went up the mountain to pay a visit. The Chan Master handed him a cushion, and the two of them sat facing each other for three days without speaking. The Chan Master was very surprised and said, "Where are you from? If you can sit peacefully without moving or having idle thoughts for three days, you are an exceptional cultivator of the Way."

Yuan replied, "Since everything is determined by fate, I crave nothing, seek nothing, and have no idle thoughts."

The Chan Master said, "I thought you were an extraordinary person, but it turns out you are just an ordinary person."

Yuan was upset and asked, "Why do you say I'm an ordinary person?"

The Master replied, "If you weren't an ordinary person, why would you allow yourself to be bound by fate?"

Yuan asked, "Is it possible to escape fate?"

He replied, "You are a scholar. The *Book of Changes* very clearly says, 'Pursue good fortune and avoid calamity.' If it were not possible to escape fate, how could we pursue good fortune and avoid calamity?"

Yuan experienced a great awakening and changed his name to Liaofan (Ending the ordinary). From that day onward, he was no longer an ordinary person. Thenceforth, he extensively practiced good deeds and accumulated a lot of merit and virtue. The diviner's words were no longer accurate. He lived to be over eighty, and had three sons. Thus, fate is not fixed, and fortune and calamity are not fixed. The ancients said, "The superior person creates his own

「君子造命」，有道德的人、正人君子，是可以改造命運，超出命數之外的。

爲什麼不吉祥？就是心裏不吉祥，種下惡因當然有惡報，要是能改過遷善，就可以趨吉避凶。從這個看來，命運是可以改造的，操之在自己手中，所謂「大善大惡，超出數外」。

destiny." People who are virtuous, wise and proper can mold their own destinies and transcend their fate.

Why is there misfortune? It's because there is misfortune in the mind. If you plant bad causes, of course there will be a bad retribution. If you can reform your faults and go toward the good, then you can pursue good fortune and avoid calamity. From this perspective, we see that fate can be changed, and the power to do so is in our own hands. As it is said, "Great good and great evil can transcend fate."

求菩薩爲全球消毒

用甘露和法水來消世界的毒氣，
消一分，世界就多得一分平安。

爲什麼打地藏七？因爲現在世界災難太多了，所
以祈禱地藏菩薩本願的力量，將一切災難消滅。

地藏菩薩所注重的就是孝道，因爲他生生世世都
是孝順父母。可是這並不容易，都是在困苦艱難
中鍛鍊出來的。他的父母不信三寶，然而他能順
承其意，用種種善巧方便法門來誘導他們生正信
三寶之心。他到處所行的菩薩道是無相無著。無
相是因他所行所作都不居功，不讚自己德行。就
算救度眾生，他也說是眾生自度的，而不要眾生
來感謝他，叩頭頂禮。

他在菩薩的行列裏，沒有覺得自己比其他的菩薩
高明，或願力大，或慈悲大，或神通廣，他沒有
這樣的想法。他的一舉一動、一言一行都是行所
無事，都認爲是自己的本分，而不居功，所以感

Asking the Bodhisattva to Disinfect the Planet

Sweet dew and Dharma-water are used to dispel the poisonous energy in the world. For each bit that is dispelled, the world obtains a bit of peace.

Why are we holding a session to recite the name of Earth Treasury Bodhisattva? It's because there are too many disasters in the world now. We want to ask Earth Treasury Bodhisattva, based on the power of his past vows, to dispel all the calamities.

What Earth Treasury Bodhisattva values most is the practice of filiality, because he was filial and compliant to his parents in life after life. But it wasn't easy—he perfected this practice by undergoing many ordeals and hardships. When his parents did not believe in the Triple Jewel, he would respect and comply with their wishes, while using various skillful and expedient Dharma-doors to lead them to have faith in the Triple Jewel. Everywhere he goes, he practices the Bodhisattva path but never gets attached to appearances. That is, he doesn't get attached to the merit of his deeds. He doesn't praise his own virtuous conduct. Even when he saves living beings, he says that the living beings saved themselves; he doesn't want living beings to thank him or bow to him.

Among the ranks of Bodhisattvas, he doesn't feel that he is more eminent than the other Bodhisattvas. He doesn't entertain the idea that his vows are bigger, or that his kindness and compassion are vaster, or that his spiritual powers are greater. No matter what he says or does, he doesn't make a big deal out of it, because he feels

動一切眾生稱揚讚歎，甚至佛也讚歎他。佛是不
隨便讚歎人的，要有值得讚歎的資格與價值才去
讚歎，因爲地藏菩薩不居功、不宣傳自己的功德
，所以感應道交。這是一種自然的感應道交，並
非用任何手段或方法而獲得的感應，而是很自然
的。所以我們人修道應學習地藏菩薩的精神與無
邊誓願：

　　　　地獄不空，誓不成佛；
　　　　眾生度盡，方證菩提。

每年我們打七，這是爲虛空世界消毒。現在世界
空氣染污，宇宙間醞釀著一種毒氣，任何方法都
無法消除，只有誠心請求諸佛菩薩放光消除這種
毒氣，把這種無影無形的戾氣消滅。所以萬佛聖
城所行所作，關係全世界的安危。這個道場的人
再不誠心，世界將更危險了！

世界人類所造的罪業太多，人的力量無法將其免
去。今天正逢地藏菩薩聖誕，大家異口同音誠念
「地藏王菩薩」，期望能感動菩薩而生慈悲心，
那麼世界就得到平安。這種感應要看我們誠心與
否？單單一人的力量是不夠的，還須大眾的力量

he is just carrying out his duty. He doesn't dwell on his own merit. For that reason, all living beings are moved to praise him, and the Buddha himself lauds him. The Buddha does not casually praise a person; he only praises those who are worthy of it. Since Earth Treasury Bodhisattva does not dwell on or advertise his own merit and virtue, he can obtain a response in the Way. Such a response comes naturally; he doesn't use any special method to obtain it. In our own cultivation, we should imitate the spirit of Earth Treasury Bodhisattva and his boundless vow:

> *As long as the hells are not empty.*
> *I vow not to become a Buddha.*
> *Only when all living beings have been saved*
> *will I accomplish Bodhi.*

Every year, we hold the session for the sake of dispelling the poisons in space and in the world. The atmosphere is now very polluted, and there is a poisonous energy brewing in the universe which can't be dispelled. We can only sincerely ask the Buddhas and Bodhisattvas to shine their light and cause the invisible but lethal toxic energy to disappear. Therefore all the activities at the City of Ten Thousand Buddhas have a direct impact on the state of peace or danger in the world. If the people in this Bodhimanda are not sincere, the world will be in even greater danger!

Mankind has committed too many offenses, and does not have the power to evade the retribution. Today, on the birthday of Earth Treasury Bodhisattva, everyone is reciting the name of Earth Treasury Bodhisattva in unison, hoping the Bodhisattva will be compassionate and cause the world to be peaceful. The possibility of such a response depends on our sincerity. One person's strength is not enough; the entire assembly's strength is required. It is said, "The unity of purpose is like a strong fortress." With united

。所以說眾志成城、群策群力，共同來祈禱世界和平。

現在的人默默中都有個感覺，都知這世界不和平，岌岌可危。所以現在所有的道場都說祈禱世界和平。最初是由佛教講堂、金山聖寺提倡，以後跟著香港、臺灣都學會了，這就證明世界就快面臨大災厄，所以要祈禱和平。可是真正祈禱世界和平的道場是萬佛聖城，為什麼？因為我們做什麼法會，並沒有希望大護法供養多少錢，每年都是無聲無息地做，到時就做。不管有沒有齋主，都照樣舉行，當成自己的本份事，而不存絲毫之企圖。我們只希望得到佛光加被，將全世界的毒氣消除；觀音菩薩用甘露水來灌頂，令眾生災消痛除，罪滅福生；地藏菩薩願力廣大，希望他使眾生離苦得樂，把災難厄劫化為烏有。念觀音菩薩、地藏菩薩是給世界消毒，不用殺蟲水，而是用甘露和法水來消世界的毒氣，消一分，世界就多得一分平安，全世界的毒氣都消了，則眾生受福，人類幸甚矣！

一九八二年地藏七 九月四日開示於萬佛聖城

strength and wisdom, let us pray for world peace together.

Nowadays, people all have the feeling that the world is not at peace, and is in fact in imminent peril. Therefore, all the temples are praying for world peace now. It was the Buddhist Lecture Hall and Gold Mountain Monastery that started it, and then the temples in Hong Kong and Taiwan followed suit. This confirms that the world is on the brink of disaster, and we must pray for peace. The Bodhimanda that is truly praying for world peace is the City of Ten Thousand Buddhas. That's because whenever we hold any Dharma event, we don't hope that a great Dharma-protector will come and give us a large donation. Every year when the time comes, we just organize the Dharma event without making a lot of commotion. We conduct the affair as usual, whether or not there is a sponsor, because we see it as our obligation and don't expect any reward for doing it. Our only hope is that the Buddha's light will aid us and purge the world of poisonous energy. We hope Guanyin Bodhisattva will anoint our crowns with sweet dew, dispel the disasters and illnesses of living beings, and cancel their sins and increase their blessings. We also hope Earth Treasury Bodhisattva, with the great strength of his vows, will enable living beings to leave suffering and attain bliss, and eradicate all calamity and peril. Reciting the names of Guanyin Bodhisattva and Earth Treasury Bodhisattva is a way to disinfect the world without the use of pesticides or chemical sprays. Rather, sweet dew and Dharma-water are used to dispel the poisonous energy in the world. For each bit that is dispelled, the world obtains a bit of peace. When all the poisonous energy has been purged from the world, living beings will be blessed and mankind will be lucky indeed!

A talk given on September 4, 1982 during an Earth Treasury
Recitation Session at the City of Ten Thousand Buddhas

什麼是佛法

修道，就是要「倒過來」。

什麼叫佛法？佛法，就是世間法；不過是世間人
所不願意行的法。世間人忙忙碌碌、奔奔波波，
出發點無非是自私，是為了保護自己的生命財產
。而佛法，是大公無私，是為了利益他人。學佛
法，一舉一動都要為他人著想，把自我看輕了，
捨己為人，不令他人生煩惱，這就是佛法。一般
人往往對於這一點認識不清楚，所以在佛教裏爭
爭吵吵、煩煩惱惱、是是非非，跟一般世俗人沒
有兩樣，甚至於有過之而無不及。一邊學佛，一
邊造罪業；一邊立功，一邊損德。這樣，對佛教
不但沒有利益，反而有大害。這就是佛所說的：
「獅子身中蟲，自食獅子肉。」

身為佛弟子，在佛教裏這麼自私自利，看不破，
放不下，怎會與佛法有所相應？學佛的人要：

What is Buddhadharma?

**Cultivating the Way simply means
to "turn ourselves around."**

What is Buddhadharma? Buddhadharma is simply worldly dharma, but it's a variety of worldly dharma that most people are unwilling to use. Worldly people are always busy running here and there, constantly hurried and agitated. The source of all this activity is invariably selfishness, motivated by a concern to protect one's life and possessions. Buddhadharma, on the other hand, is unselfish and public-spirited, and springs from a wish to benefit others. As we learn the Buddhadharma, our every action gradually comes to include in its scope a concern for others. The ego gradually loses its importance. We should give up our own interests in service to others, and avoid bringing affliction to others. These are the hallmarks of Buddhadharma. But most people fail to clearly understand these basic ideas. As a result, within Buddhist circles we find struggle and contention, troubles and hassles, quarrels and strife. We find an atmosphere not at all different from that of ordinary people. Sometimes the relationships within Buddhist groups don't even measure up to the standards of ordinary social conduct. Such people study Buddhism on the one hand and create offenses on the other. They do good deeds, and in the next breath destroy the merit and virtue they've earned. Instead of advancing the cause of Buddhism, such behavior actually harms it. The

> 眞認自己錯，
>
> 莫論他人非；
>
> 他非即我非，
>
> 同體名大悲。

要徹底瞭解佛教的眞理，自己必須先要修忍辱、布施，才能有所成就。必須要「翻過來」，這也就是與世俗的人有所不同，不要同流合污。修道，就是要「倒過來」，這是什麼意思呢？就是「好事給他人，壞事與自己。」捨棄小我，完成大我。

你們皈依我的人，都是我身上的血和肉。無論把哪一塊肉割去，都是很痛的。無論哪一個地方流血，元氣都會受損傷的，所以你們要互相團結。爲了要使佛教發揚光大，就要吃人所不願意吃的虧，受人所不能受的侮辱。心量要放大，行爲要眞實。如果不向眞的去做，佛菩薩是知道的，我們不能欺騙佛菩薩。大家要檢討己過，痛改前非，眞正認識自己以往的顛倒和不合理的作風。要老老實實，忘記自己，而爲整個佛教、整個社會服務。

Buddha referred to such people as "parasites on the lion, feeding off the lion's flesh."

We Buddhist disciples cannot expect any results from our cultivation if we're selfish and profiteering, unable to put things down and see through our attachments. The motto of Buddhists must be:

> *Truly recognize your own faults,*
> *And don't discuss others' wrongs.*
> *Others' wrongs are just my own:*
> *Being of one substance with all things*
> *is called Great Compassion.*

If we want to thoroughly understand the truths of Buddhism, then we must first cultivate patience and giving. Then we can come to accomplishment. We must turn ourselves around and be different from ordinary people. We can no longer flow along with the turbid currents of the world. Cultivating the Way simply means to "turn ourselves around." What is that? It means to "give desirable situations and benefits to other people, while absorbing the unfavorable situations ourselves." We renounce the petty self in order to bring to perfection the greater self.

All disciples who have taken refuge with me are like the flesh and blood of my own body. No matter which piece of flesh is severed from my body, it hurts me just the same. No matter where I bleed, the wound injures my constitution. Because of this, all of you must unite together. To make Buddhism expand and flourish, you must take a loss in places where most people are unable to sustain a loss.

本來在世界上，無論哪一個團體，哪一個社會，都是錯綜複雜，互相勾心鬥角。在金山聖寺、萬佛聖城、金輪聖寺，以及隸屬法界佛教總會的所有道場，都要把這種情形改善。當然，不能馬上改得很圓滿，可是也要一步一步做去，改到最圓滿、最徹底、最究竟的地步。然後，還要念茲在茲保存這種良好的行為、志願，去推展佛教，令佛教發揚光大。這是每個佛弟子應有的責任。佛教若不興旺，乃是因為我本人沒有盡到責任。不要把責任推諉到他人身上。若能這樣，不久的將來，佛教一定能發揚光大，推行到世界每一個角落！

身為佛弟子，天天求佛庇佑，不外求佛幫助我，或者助我發財，或者助我陞官，或者助我開智慧——只知道求佛幫助自己，但沒有想想我們對佛教有什麼貢獻？是不是拿出真心來？就在這個地方我們要常常迴光返照。

皈依時發菩薩四宏誓願：

You must endure the insults that ordinary people find unendurable. Expand the measure of your minds, and be true in your actions. When you're not trying to be true, the Buddhas and Bodhisattvas are aware of it. No one can cheat them. Each of you should examine your own faults and earnestly remedy the flaws in your character. Truly recognize where in the past you've been upside-down and where your behavior has departed from principle. Be honest, forget about yourself, and work for the sake of all of Buddhism and all of society.

No matter where you look in the world, every organization and every society has its own complications and power struggles. At Gold Mountain Monastery, Gold Wheel Monastery, the City of Ten Thousand Buddhas, and the other Way-places that belong to the Dharma Realm Buddhist Association, we must correct these faults. Naturally we can't expect perfection immediately, but we can hope to improve step by step. We can change things until we reach the ultimate point of perfection. Then in thought after thought, we must preserve this wholesome behavior and maintain our resolve and purpose as we go about disseminating Buddhism, so that its light spreads far and wide. All disciples of the Buddha share this responsibility equally. We must think, "If Buddhism fails to flourish, I haven't fulfilled my responsibility." Don't pass your duty to others. If we can shoulder our responsibility in this way, then in the near future, Buddhism will certainly expand and spread to every corner of the world!

As Buddhist disciples, do we seek the Buddhas' aid every day? Do we pray that the Buddha will help us get rich, help us rise to power, or help us develop wisdom? Are we concerned only with personal

（一）眾生無邊誓願度。問問自己：「我度了眾生嗎？」若度了，不妨再多度一點；若沒有度，就要趕快發心度眾生。

（二）煩惱無盡誓願斷。煩惱是無窮無盡的，但要把它反過來，化爲菩提。反過來沒有？若還沒有，就快點把它反過來。

（三）法門無量誓願學。自我檢討：有沒有學佛法？有沒有爲佛教出點力？是不是學了死死板板的佛法，不懂得活用，一日曝之，十日寒之？

（四）佛道無上誓願成。天下沒有比佛道更超脫、更究竟的法門。我有沒有眞正發願去成佛？不但是自己成佛，還要度一切眾生成佛！

且看，釋迦牟尼佛往昔「三祇修福慧，百劫種相好。」爲半句偈而捨生命，這種精神是多麼偉大！爲法之誠，多麼高超！大家要效法這種精神。

advantages? Do we forget all about making a contribution to Buddhism? Have we brought forth a genuine resolve or not? Right at this point we must reflect inwardly. When we took refuge with the Triple Jewel, we made the four vast vows of Bodhisattvas:

1. *Living beings are numberless, I vow to save them all.* Ask yourself, "Have I saved any living beings?" If so, then why not save a few more? And if not, then all the more reason to quickly resolve to rescue living beings.
2. *Afflictions are infinite, I vow to cut them off.* There is a limitless quantity of afflictions, but we must reverse them, transform them into Bodhi. "Have I reversed them?" If not, then quickly turn them over right away!
3. *Dharma-doors are measureless, I vow to learn them all.* Ask yourself, "Have I learned any of the Buddhadharma? Have I brought forth the slightest bit of strength for Buddhism? Have I been too rigid and inflexible in my study of the teachings? Isn't it the case that my study of Dharma-doors is off and on?"
4. *The Buddha's Way is supreme, I vow to realize it.* There is no dharma on earth that surpasses the Buddha's Way, nor one that is more ultimate. Have I really made a resolve to accomplish Buddhahood? What's more, we shouldn't resolve to accomplish Buddhahood for ourselves alone, but to take all living beings across to Buddhahood.

In the past, Shakyamuni Buddha "cultivated blessings and wisdom for three great innumerable eons, and developed the fine features and hallmarks for one hundred eons." He gave up his life for half a verse of Dharma. How great his spirit was! His sincerity in seeking the Dharma was truly noble. We should all imitate his model of

洛杉磯的金輪聖寺，我每個月來一次，差不多有三、四年了。我覺得你們每個人沒有從佛法得到真正的利益，沒有真正體會到佛法偉大的精神。還是把自己畫到佛法的外邊去，未能深入。

要想佛教興盛，首先要從自己身上做起，要獻出真心，為佛教犧牲、努力，不要在小圈子裏混。應以法界為體，虛空為用，「應無所住而生其心」，每個人果真能這樣，那麼佛教就會發達。

vigor. I come to Gold Wheel Monastery in Los Angeles once a month, and have done so for nearly four years. I feel that none of you has gained any genuine benefit from the Dharma. You haven't truly experienced the greatness of the Buddhadharma's spirit. Instead you have placed yourselves outside the Buddhadharma, without being able to deeply enter it.

Our attitude should be, "If Buddhism is going to flourish, then it must begin with my own person." What we need are true hearts, endowed with a genuine spirit of devotion to the Buddhadharma. Work hard and break free of the small circles that you've drawn around yourselves. Take the entire Dharma Realm as your own body! Let all of empty space be your field of action! This means, "bring forth thoughts that linger nowhere." If every person would really do this, then Buddhism could truly flourish in this country.

迴向偈

願以此功德　莊嚴佛淨土
上報四重恩　下濟三途苦
若有見聞者　悉發菩提心
盡此一報身　同生極樂國

Verse of Transference

May the merit and virtue accrued from this work
Adorn the Buddhas' Pure Lands,
Repaying four kinds of kindness above
And aiding those suffering in the paths below.
May those who see and hear of this
All bring forth the resolve for Bodhi
And, when this retribution body is over,
Be born together in the Land of Ultimate Bliss.

附錄
Appendix

辭彙解釋
Glossary

宣化上人簡傳
Biographical Sketch of the
Venerable Master Hsüan Hua

Glossary

This glossary is an aid for readers unfamiliar with the Buddhist vocabulary. Definitions have been kept simple, and are not necessarily complete.

Amitabha Buddha 阿彌陀佛 See Land of Ultimate Bliss.

Amitabha Buddha recitation session 彌陀七 A retreat, usually lasting seven days, during which participants practice mindful recitation, whether aloud or silently, of Amitabha Buddha's name all day long.

Arhat 阿羅漢 One of the fruitions of the path of cultivation. Arhats have attained the cessation of involuntary physical birth and death. The word has three meanings, which are as follows:

1. Worthy of offerings.
2. Killer of thieves. Arhats have killed the thieves of afflictions and outflows.
3. Without birth. An Arhat dwells in the forbearance of the non-arising of dharmas. They have ended birth and death of the body.

Bhikshu 比丘 A fully ordained Buddhist monk, one who leads a pure and celibate life and upholds 250 precepts.

Bhikshuni 比丘尼 A fully ordained Buddhist nun, one who leads a pure life and upholds 348 precepts. The feminine form of Bhikshu.

Bodhi 菩提 Enlightenment.

Bodhimanda 道場 A place where enlightenment is sought and attained; a Way-place.

Bodhisattva 菩薩 An enlightened being who does not enter Nirvana but chooses instead to remain in the world and save living beings.

Bodhi resolve 菩提心 A resolve to seek enlightenment by cultivating the spiritual path.

Buddha 佛 The Enlightened One, one who has reached the Utmost, Right, and Equal Enlightenment. Buddhahood is inherent in all beings. As long as it remains unrealized, they remain beings; once it is realized, they are Buddhas.

Buddhadharma 佛法 Methods of cultivation taught by the Buddha leading beings to enlightenment.

Chan 禪 One of the five major schools of Buddhism. The teaching of meditation. Also, the Chinese transliteration of Dhyana.

Chan session 禪七 A retreat, usually lasting a multiple of seven days, during which participants practice sitting and walking meditation all day long.

cultivation 修行 The practical application of the methods taught by the Buddha that lead to enlightenment.

cultivator 修行人 One who cultivates (see cultivation).

Dharma 法 The teachings of the Buddha, also called Buddha-dharma. After the Buddha's Nirvana, the Dharma passes through the following historical periods:

1. The first 1000 years is the Proper Dharma Age
2. The following 1,000 years is the Dharma Image Age
3. The following 10,000 years is the Dharma Ending Age

dharma 法 An element of psycho-physical existence; a method of cultivation.

Dharma-door 法門 An entrance to the Dharma, a method of practice leading to enlightenment.

Dharma Master 法師 A teacher of Dharma. A polite term of address for members of the Sangha.

Dharma Realm 法界 (1) The enlightened world, that is, the totality or infinity of the realm of the Buddhas; (2) a particular plane of existence, as in the Ten Dharma Realms; or (3) the eighteenth of the Eighteen Sense-fields, which refers to the objects of the mind.

Dharma-Selecting Eye 擇法眼 The ability to discriminate the Proper Dharma from deviant doctrines.

Dhyana 禪 A practice of thought cultivation and insight which leads to the development of higher mental states.

(Those) Enlightened to Conditions 緣覺 Pratyekabuddhas, those who attain enlightenment through contemplation of the twelve links of conditioned co-production.

Earth Treasury Bodhisattva 地藏菩薩 One of the greatest of the Bodhisattvas. He is renowned as foremost in the conduct of saving beings.

externalist way 外道 Heterodox sects; non-ultimate teachings that seek outside the mind.

five precepts 五戒 The five lay precepts are: no killing, no stealing, no sexual misconduct, no false speech, and no intoxicants.

Four Vast Vows 四宏誓願 The vows made by those who aspire to practice the Bodhisattva Path: (1) I vow to save the limitless living beings; (2) I vow to cut off the inexhaustible afflictions; (3) I vow to study the immeasurable Dharma doors. (4) I vow to realize the supreme Buddha Way.

Four-fold Assembly 四眾 The assembly of Bhikshus, Bhikshunis, Upasakas, and Upasikas.

Great Compassion Mantra 大悲咒 One of the most widely used and most efficacious of all Buddhist mantras, the Great Compassion Mantra is a dharma taught by the Bodhisattva Who Regards the Sounds of the World (see Guanshiyin Bodhisattva). The teachings on the Great Compassion Mantra are found in the *Dharani Sutra*.

Great Vehicle 大乘 See Mahayana.

Guanshiyin/Guanyin Bodhisattva 觀世音菩薩 The Bodhisattva of Great Compassion Who Regards the Sounds of the World. "Guanshiyin" is a Chinese transliteration of the Bodhisattva's Sanskrit name, Avalokiteshvara.

Han Yü 韓愈 A famous poet and philosopher of the Tang dynasty, A.D. 768–824.

karma 業 Deeds, activity. Karma does not mean fate. It means the deeds which we create ourselves and the retributions which those deeds bring upon us.

Land of Ultimate Bliss 極樂世界 The Buddhaland of Amitabha Buddha in the West created through the power of his vows which enable living beings to be reborn simply by constant mindfulness and recitation of his name.

leave home 出家 To renounce the householder's life and become a monk or nun in order to devote oneself completely to the practice of the Buddhadharma.

Manjushri Bodhisattva 文殊師利菩薩 One of the greatest of the Bodhisattvas. He is renowned as foremost in wisdom.

six paths of rebirth 六道 See Ten Dharma Realms.

six spiritual powers 六種神通 The heavenly eye, heavenly ear, knowledge of previous lives, knowledge of the minds of others, complete spirit, and elimination of outflows.

Sumeru 須彌 The axial mountain in the center of every world system.

Sutra 經 Discourses by the Buddha or by various members of the assembly with the authority of the Buddha.

Tathagata 如來 One of the titles of the Buddha. Tathagata means Thus Come One.

Ten Dharma Realms 十法界 The four realms of the sages (Buddhas, Bodhisattvas, Those Enlightened to Conditions, and Hearers) and the six paths of rebirth (gods, humans, asuras, animals, hungry ghosts, and hell-beings).

ten good deeds 十善 Abstention from: killing, stealing, sexual misconduct, duplicity, harsh speech, lying, irrresponsible speech, greed, anger, and stupidity.

three evil paths 三惡道 The realms of animals, hungry ghosts, and hell-beings.

Three Treasuries 三藏 the Sutras, the Vinaya (rules of discipline), and the Shastras (discourses by later masters)

Twelve Divisions of the Canon 十二部 Twelve types of Sutra text, namely: prose, verses, predictions, isolated incidents, unrequested teachings, causes and conditions, analogies, past lives, lives of disciples, extensive teachings, previously non-existent Dharma, and discussions.

Triple Jewel 三寶 The Buddha, the Dharma, and the Sangha.

Triple Realm 三界 The Realm of Desire, the Realm of Form, and the Formless Realm.

Universal Worthy Bodhisattva 普賢菩薩 One of the greatest of the Bodhisattvas. He is renowned as foremost in making vast vows.

Upasaka, Upasika 優婆塞、優婆夷 Respectively a layman and laywoman who have taken refuge with the Triple Jewel.

Vajra 金剛 A Sanskrit word which means "durable," "luminous," and "able to cut." It is indestructible, and is usually represented by diamond.

Way 道 The spiritual path of cultivation; the ultimate truth, which is realized through following that path.

Way-place 道場 See Bodhimanda.

宣化上人簡傳

上人，法名安慈，字度輪，接雲公法，為禪宗溈仰派第九代傳人，法號宣化，又號「墓中僧」。吉林省雙城縣人，清末戊午年三月十六日生。俗姓白，父富海，母胡氏。上人的母親一生茹素念佛，懷上人時曾向佛菩薩祈願，生上人前夕，夢見阿彌陀佛大放光明，遂生上人。

幼年時代，上人隨母親茹素念佛，年十一，見生死事大，無常迅速，毅然有出家之志，十五歲皈依上常下智老和尚為師。十九歲母親逝世，禮請三緣寺上常下智老和尚為剃度，披緇結廬於母墓旁，守孝期間，拜華嚴、禮淨懺、修禪定、習教觀，嚴守日中一食，功夫日純，得到鄉里人民的愛戴禮敬，其洗鍊精虔，感動諸佛菩薩、護法龍天，故靈異之事多不勝數，神異事蹟廣傳，被稱為奇僧。

一九四六年，因慕虛雲老和尚為宗門泰斗，乃前

Biographical Sketch of the Venerable Master Hsuan Hua

The Venerable Master, whose Dharma name is An Tse and style name is Du Lun, received the Dharma from the Venerable Master Hsu Yun and became the Ninth Patriarch of the Wei Yang Lineage. His name is Hsuan Hua, and he is also called The Monk in the Grave. A native of Shuangcheng County of Jilin Province, he was born on the sixteenth day of the third lunar month in the year of Wu Wu at the end of the Qing Dynasty. His father's name was Bai Fuhai. His mother, whose maiden name was Hu, ate only vegetarian food and recited the Buddha's name throughout her life. When she was pregnant with the Master, she prayed to the Buddhas and Bodhisattvas. The night before his birth, in a dream, she saw Amitabha Buddha emitting brilliant light. Following that the Master was born.

As a child, the Master followed his mother's example and ate only vegetarian food and recited the Buddha's name. At the age of eleven, he became aware of the great matter of birth and death and the brevity of life and resolved to leave the home-life. At fifteen, he took refuge under the Venerable Master Chang Zhi. When he was nineteen, his mother passed away, and he requested Venerable Master Chang Zhi of Sanyuan Temple to shave his head. Dressed in the left-home robes, he built a simple hut by his mother's grave and observed the practice of filial piety. During that period, he bowed to the *Avatamsaka Sutra,* performed worship and pure repentance, practiced Chan meditation, studied the teachings and contemplations, and strictly kept the rule of eating only one meal at midday. As his skill grew ever more pure, he won the admiration and respect of the villagers. His intensely sincere efforts to purify and cultivate himself moved the Buddhas and Bodhisattvas as well

往參禮。虛雲老和尚觀其爲法門龍象，乃傳授其法脈，爲溈仰宗第九代接法人，爲摩訶迦葉初祖傳承的四十六代。

一九四八年，叩別虛雲老和尚，赴香港弘法，闡揚禪、教、律、密、淨五宗並重，打破門戶之見。並重建古刹、印經造像，分別成立西樂園寺、佛教講堂、慈興寺，開演經典多部，使佛法大興於香江。

一九五九年，師觀察西方機緣成熟，爲將佛教的眞實義理傳到世界各地，遂令弟子在美成立中美佛教總會﹝後改爲法界佛教總會﹞。一九六二年，應美國佛敎人士邀請，隻身赴美，樹正法幢於三藩市佛教講堂。

一九六八年，成立暑假楞嚴講修班，數十名華盛頓州立大學學生，遠來學習佛法。結業後，美籍青年五人，懇求剃度出家，創下美國佛教史始有僧相的記錄。此後，在上人座下披剃的美國弟子

responses were too many to be counted. As news of these supernatural events spread far and wide, the Master came to be regarded as a remarkable monk.

Esteeming the Venerable Master Hsu Yun as a great hero of Buddhism, the Master went to pay homage to him in 1946. The Venerable Master Hsu Yun saw that the Master would become an outstanding figure in the Dharma, and transmitted the Dharma-pulse to him, making him the Ninth Patriarch of the Wei Yang Lineage, the forty-sixth generation since the Patriarch Mahakashyapa.

In 1948, the Master bid farewell to the Venerable Master Hsu Yun and went to Hong Kong to propagate the Dharma. He gave equal importance to the five schools—Chan, Doctrine, Vinaya, Esoteric, and Pure Land—thus putting an end to prejudice towards any particular sect. The Master also renovated old temples, printed Sutras and constructed images. He established Western Bliss Garden Monastery, the Buddhist Lecture Hall, and Cixing Monastery. Delivering lectures on numerous Sutras, the Master caused Buddhism to flourish in Hong Kong.

In 1959, the Master saw that conditions were ripe in the West, and he instructed his disciples to establish the Sino-American Buddhist Association (later renamed the Dharma Realm Buddhist Association) in the United States. In 1962, at the invitation of American Buddhists, the Master traveled alone to the United States, where he raised the banner of proper Dharma at the Buddhist Lecture Hall in San Francisco.

In 1968, the Shurangama Study and Practice Summer Session was held, and several dozen students from the University of Washington in Seattle came to study the Buddhadharma. After the session was concluded, five young Americans requested permission to shave

日多，對佛法弘揚於西方及翻譯經典，都帶來深遠的影響。

上人講經說法，深入淺出，數十年如一日，升座說法萬餘次，現已有百餘種譯爲英文，爲佛經譯爲英文最多者。一九七三年成立國際譯經學院，預計將《大藏經》譯成各國文字，使佛法傳遍寰宇。

一九七四年，購置萬佛聖城，成立法界佛教大學、僧伽居士訓練班，培育國際性佛學專才。又創辦育良小學、培德中學，以教育來挽救人心。數年來相繼成立金山聖寺、金輪聖寺、金峰聖寺、金佛聖寺、華嚴聖寺、法界聖寺、彌陀聖寺、法界聖城等正法道場多處。上人本著捨己爲人之精神，不辭勞苦，以身作則，辦校演教，提拔後秀，獻出萬佛聖城爲「全世界佛教徒皈依處」。萬佛聖城家風嚴峻，堅守上人自出家以來的六大宗旨：不爭、不貪、不求、不自私、不自利、不打妄語的原則。由於上人人格與修行的感召，萬佛聖城已成爲美國佛教重要的道場。

their heads and leave the home-life, marking the beginning of the Sangha in the history of American Buddhism. Since then, the number of American disciples who have left the home-life under the Venerable Master has continued to grow, creating a profound and far-reaching impact on the propagation of the Buddhadharma and the translation of Sutras in the West.

The Master's explanations of Sutras and lectures on Dharma are profound and yet easy to understand. Several decades have passed in a flash, and the Master has ascended the Dharma seat and delivered well over ten thousand Dharma lectures. Over a hundred of his explanations have been translated into English. No one else has overseen the translation of so many Sutras into English. In 1973 the Master established the International Translation Institute, which plans to translate the entire Buddhist Canon into the languages of every country, so that the Buddhadharma will spread throughout the world.

In 1974, the Master purchased the City of Ten Thousand Buddhas and established the Dharma Realm Buddhist University and the Sangha and Laity Training Programs in order to train Buddhist professionals on an international scale. Furthermore, he founded Instilling Goodness Elementary School and Developing Virtue Secondary School in order to save children's minds from corruption. Over subsequent years, the Master has successively established Gold Mountain Monastery, Gold Wheel Monastery, Gold Summit Monastery, Gold Buddha Monastery, Avatamsaka Monastery, Dharma Realm Monastery, Amitabha Monastery, the City of the Dharma Realm, and other Way-places of the proper Dharma. Dedicating himself to serving others, the Master doesn't mind the toil and suffering. Acting as a model for others in founding schools and expounding the teachings, and in order to promote the talent of future generations, the Master has offered the City of Ten Thousand Buddhas as the "Refuge for the Buddhists of the World." The traditions at the City of Ten Thousand Buddhas

上人曾撰一聯以明其志：

> 凍死不攀緣，
> 餓死不化緣，
> 窮死不求緣。
> 隨緣不變，不變隨緣，
> 抱定我們三大宗旨。
>
> 捨命為佛事，
> 造命為本事，
> 正命為僧事。
> 即事明理，明理即事，
> 推行祖師一脈心傳。

上人甚深的禪定與智慧，實為末法眾生開出菩提大道，猶如在黑夜中見般若之燈，在黑暗裏聞法嗣之香，在污泥穢地間開起清淨之蓮，令人動容讚歎，知道偉大的修行人不可思議。

are strict, and residents vigorously strive to practice the Six Great Principles established by the Master after he left the home-life: do not contend, do not be greedy, do not seek, do not be selfish, do not pursue personal gain, and do not tell lies. Due to the influence of the Venerable Master's integrity and cultivation, the City of Ten Thousand Buddhas has become an important Buddhist Way-place in the United States. The Master has composed a verse expressing his principles:

> *Freezing to death, we do not scheme.*
> *Starving to death, we do not beg.*
> *Dying of poverty, we ask for nothing.*
> *According with conditions, we do not change.*
> *Not changing, we accord with conditions.*
> *We adhere firmly to our three great principles.*

> *We renounce our lives to do the Buddha's work.*
> *We take the responsibility to mold our own destinies.*
> *We rectify our lives as the Sangha's work.*
> *Encountering specific matters,*
>   *we understand the principles.*
> *Understanding the principles, we apply*
>   *them in specific matters.*
> *We carry on the single pulse of the patriarchs'*
>   *mind-transmission.*

The Venerable Master's profound samadhi and wisdom have truly opened up the great way of Bodhi for living beings in the age of the Dharma's decline. It is as if in the dark night, we suddenly see the lamp of Prajna wisdom, and in the obscurity, we smell the fragrance of the Dharma lineage. It is like a pure lotus which grows out of the mud and blooms. Upon realizing the inconceivable state of a great cultivator, we are moved to express our praise and exaltation.

南無護法韋陀菩薩
Namo Dharma Protector Wei Tuo Bodhisattva

法界佛教總會・萬佛聖城
Dharma Realm Buddhist Association
The City of Ten Thousand Buddhas
2001 Talmage Road, Talmage, CA 95481-0217 U.S.A.
Tel:(707)462-0939

法界聖城　The City of the Dharma Realm
1029 West Capitol Ave., West Sacramento, CA 95691 U.S.A.
Tel:(916)374-8268

國際譯經學院 The International Translation Institute
1777 Murchison Drive, Burlingame, CA 94010-4504 U.S.A.
Tel: (650)692-5912　Fax: (650)692-5056

法界宗教研究院（柏克萊寺）
Institute for World Religions (Berkeley Buddhist Monastery)
2304 McKinley Avenue, Berkeley, CA 94703 U.S.A.
Tel: (510)848-3440　Fax: (510)548-4551

金山聖寺　Gold Mountain Monastery
800 Sacramento Street, San Francisco, CA 94108 U.S.A.
Tel: (415)421-6117

金輪聖寺　Gold Wheel　Monastery
235 North Avenue 58, Los Angeles, CA 90042 U.S.A.
Tel: (213)258-6668

長堤聖寺　Long Beach Monastery
3361 East Ocean Boulevard, Long Beach, CA 90803 U.S.A.
Tel: (562)438-8902

金佛聖寺　Gold Buddha Monastery
301 East Hastings Street, Vancouver, BC V6A 1P3 CANADA
Tel: (604)684-3754

華嚴聖寺　Avatamsaka Monastery
1009-4th Avenue, S.W. Calgary, AB T2P 0K8 CANADA
Tel: (403)269-2960

法界佛教印經會
Dharma Realm Buddhist Books Distribution Society
臺灣省臺北市忠孝東路六段 85 號 11 樓
11th Floor, No.85, Sec. 6 Chung-Hsiao E. Road,
Taipei, Taiwan, R. O. C.
Tel: (02)2786-3022, 2786-2474　Fax: (02)2786-2674

紫雲洞觀音寺　Tze Yun Tung Temple
Batu 5 1/2, Jalan Sungai Besi, Salak Selatan,
57100 Kuala Lumpur, MALAYSIA.
Tel: (03)782-6560　Fax: (03)780-1272

宣化上人開示錄(一)

西曆二〇〇〇年三月廿四日‧中英文版‧平裝本
佛曆三〇二七年二月十九日‧觀音菩薩聖誕

發 行 人	法界佛教總會
出　　版	法界佛教總會‧佛經翻譯委員會‧法界佛教大學
地　　址	**Dharma Realm Buddhist Association &** **The City of Ten Thousand Buddhas** 2001 Talmage Road, Talmage, CA 95481-0217　U.S.A. 電話：(707)462-0939　　傳眞：(707)462-0949

The International Translation Institute
1777 Murchison Drive Burlingame, CA 94010-4504 U.S.A.
電話：(650)692-5912　傳眞：(650)692-5056

倡　　印	萬佛聖城 **The City of Ten Thousand Buddhas** 2001 Talmage Road, Talmage, CA 95481-0217　U.S.A. 電話：(707)462-0939　　傳眞：(707)462-0949

ISBN-0-88139-025-9

●佛典所在，即佛所在，請恭敬尊重，廣爲流通。